Living In a Box

By
Keri Chambers

British Library Cataloguing in Publication Data.
A catalogue record for this book is available from the British Library

ISBN 978 0 86071 679 2

Published on behalf of the Author by

MOORLEYS
Print, Design & Publishing
info@moorleys.co.uk · www.moorleys.co.uk

Acknowledgements

To my dear friend Shirley who has helped me enormously with editing my book.

To my parents for standing by me, giving me ideas of what I can include in my book and all the finer details I couldn't remember.

Contents

Graduation

September 2010

Yes! I had made it through my Mathematics and Statistics degree and my results had come today. As a result of being blind I had to get my Mum to read the results to me. Mum was so excited for me that her hands were shaking as she opened the envelope with my results in. Usually it says on the front page that you have passed, and then you have to look at a grid provided that lists the modules and shows what percentage you have achieved. I asked Mum to read the grid out to me but she didn't need to since it told her on the front page so Mum said, "It says here that you got a first class degree."

I then asked Mum, "Really?" and Mum replied, "Well that is what it says!"

Mum was so pleased for me that she forgot to take all the stuff she needed to a hospital appointment. That evening I went out with my Mum, Dad and older brother for a meal to celebrate.

November 2010

After all that hard work I was finally there! Today was my graduation day. I was slightly nervous, not having graduated before, but come to that, nobody in my immediate family had graduated, so it was a first time for us all. There were elements of the day I knew about from what I had arranged, but other elements I didn't know anything about. I had previously chosen what photo pack I would have and I had hired the gown. I knew that I would go up on stage to receive the certificate but I didn't know in what order students went up, or if they said something about the students before they went up on stage.

Today we had the photographers from the Derby Evening Telegraph coming to take a photo of the whole family to put in the paper. Despite it being November the weather wasn't too bad! It was foggy and frosty but at least it wasn't raining or snowing, as we had the photo taken outside. Luckily, we weren't out there too long! After they had gone my granddad came ready for us to drive up to Sheffield for my graduation. Where the graduation ceremony was being held you had to go down a one-way system. We ended up going round the one-way system 3 times trying to find the venue! We even asked a traffic warden if he could come in the car to show us the way. Eventually we got there and got parked up.

At the graduation venue I got gowned up, although the mortar board that I had hired did not fit so they had to find me a bigger one. It wasn't a surprise that I had a big head—we already knew that! I then had my photographs taken before going to have some more photos taken for the Sheffield newspaper.

I had previously thought that we would line up in alphabetical order for each subject and then we would be lead into the ceremony in time for us to go up on stage, but it wasn't like that.

At the graduation ceremony all the guests sat in one area whilst all the students sat together somewhere else, waiting to be called up on stage. I had already arranged that I would sit with the other students with two of my personal assistants, who would take me up on stage, to receive my certificate. Whilst I was waiting to go up on stage I kept thinking of my grandparents who are dead and wishing that they could be here watching me and what they would have said, but I knew they would be up there watching me anyway. It was surprising just how many students were graduating that day and the ceremony seemed to stretch on for ages whilst I waited for them to call my name, but finally it was time for me to go up on stage to receive my certificate. When I was walking to the stage I was so excited but I kept thinking "Oh please don't let me fall over in my gown in front of all the guests"—it would have been really embarrassing and I would have looked a right Charlie! Up on stage I received my certificate and shook hands with the Vice Chancellor before going back down the steps off stage, once again I hoped I wouldn't fall. Thankfully I got back to where I was sitting without any mishaps and waited for the rest of the students to go up.

After the ceremony we all went back to the university where we got the chance to talk to the tutors. At the university all the students who had graduated in Maths got together and we threw our hats up in the air. As I threw my hat up in the air, I felt a rush of exhilaration. This was a feeling I had never experienced before, a feeling that was clearly displayed across my face, for the world to see!

After this we went for a celebratory meal with my two personal assistants and the two people that supported me through my degree. Not too far from the university was a little Italian restaurant where we went for the meal. At the restaurant we were directed to a large table, with me sat at the head.

Whilst sitting at the head of the table, I smiled to myself as I thought of how proud my family and granddad were that I had graduated, I also thought of my other grandparents, who I really wished could have been there with me to celebrate. I was so proud of myself and what I had achieved despite my difficulties, knowing that I had proved to the world that people who had health problems were as capable as anybody else and could still work towards reaching their ambition.

Chapter 1

Winters Gone By

December, cold nights with frost on the grass making it look pastel green. Snow wrapping the landscape in white bringing with it a peaceful and bright quality. Or, at least, that was how it was when I was little before the weather changed to mild, wet and windy.

Loving the snow when it came to set in for winter, often bringing down the power lines and making us rely on floating candles to provide light for meals and reading. Once when it had snowed heavily and we were eating dinner by candle light I said, "Isn't this romantic Mummy!"

And Mum said, "Something beginning with r!"

I remember building snowmen in our back garden, when we had lots of snow, and playing in the snow. I spent a lot of time clearing the snow off our drive so Dad could park the car there when he came home from work. One time it had snowed I was clearing the snow off the drive with Alex and two friends and we hadn't long finished clearing it when it snowed again, so we cleared it again but it snowed again. After the third time of clearing the snow for more snow to come we gave it up as a bad job! When Dad came home from work he said, "I thought you would have cleared the snow off the drive," and we said, "We did 3 times, but it kept snowing!"

Dad had built a sledge for us and we went sledging at Wollaton Park, down the grassy slopes, but I used to get upset when the sledge went down a dip and I fell off. Once we went to have a look at another slope near us and Dad said, "I will go down first to check it is okay." So Dad went down first. When he was going down the slope everything was okay up until one bit where the sledge caught on a hummock and stopped, but Dad carried on falling. Well Mum, Alex and I were helpless with laughter when Dad came back to us and said, "I could be really badly hurt and all you 3 can do is laugh!" Needless to say we didn't go sledging there!
Now when it snows, because I can't see the snow, I enjoy going out for walks in it, so I can feel it under my feet and falling on me and I can

appreciate it that way. I don't really mind falling in the snow, especially if it is fresh snow because it's nice and soft, but I can't get straight up off my bottom but have to roll on to my hands and knees and push myself up that way, due to my poor balance. The trouble is, if I roll onto my hands and knees in the snow I get more of myself wet than I like, so somebody else has to pull me up!

Once when it had snowed I went for a walk with Mum and I was pushing my cane through the snow. At one point my cane went down a hole and I think "Blimey that is a steep step" then I realise my cane has gone down a grate!

When Alex and I were little we used to listen to Christmas songs on tape or CD from October right through until Christmas, but now we only start listening to Christmas music from Armistice Day.

I love listening to Christmas songs and thinking about what the song means to me whilst I am singing to the music. A lot of Christmas songs put pictures in my head like the song: 'Mistletoe and Wine', by Cliff Richard where he sings 'logs on the fire' which makes me think of a cosy lounge where people are sitting in front of a fire and the logs are burning with a reddish glow. The part 'gifts on the tree' makes me think of that picture with a Christmas tree in front of the window.

'I'm Dreaming of a White Christmas' when he sings 'where treetops glisten and children listen to hear sleigh bells in the snow' makes me think of a winter scene of a Christmas tree shining in the sunlight/moonlight with snow on it and children playing nearby listening to sleigh bells.

'Let it Snow' when he sings 'the weather outside is frightful but the fire is so delightful' and 'the lamps are turned down low' make me think of a lounge where you can see it snowing outside in the evening when it is dark and a crackling fire in a lamp lit room.

Part of the music of 'Saviour's Day' by Cliff Richard makes me think of a landscape scene of mountains where a river is cascading down a waterfall.

The song 'Snow is falling' when he sings 'under the mistletoe and kiss by candle light' puts a picture of a man and woman kissing under a sprig of mistletoe in a room lit by candles and a Christmas tree.

'When the snowman brings the snow' when they sing 'let the bells ring out for Christmas' makes me think of a snow-covered village with a church where the bells are ringing on Christmas Eve.

I used to love December, the excitement of the approach of Christmas, counting down the days on my advent calendar, wondering each morning what would be behind each window. As my vision got worse Mum used to have to go over the numbers in thick felt-tip so I could see the numbers and open them myself. Once my vision got really bad Mum used to have to find the numbers for me so I could open the doors. It wasn't until I was about 20 that Mum and Dad saw the material advent calendars with the pockets round the edges. Now all Mum has to do is put the chocolates in the pockets and I can get one out each morning. The great thing about this is you can put whatever chocolate you want in the pockets! I could have done with the material advent calendars years ago!

The first weekend in December always used to be exciting when Mum and Dad got the Christmas decorations out to put up. Alex and I used to love decorating the Christmas tree with all the baubles and tinsel. Now we enjoy putting the Christmas window clings on our windows and doors even though Mum has to come round and straighten them.

Even when Alex's and my vision started deteriorating Santa always used to buy us things we wanted that we could still see to do. The writing on the labels attached to Christmas presents from Santa used to be as big as what we needed, clever! It never used to surprise me that Santa knew what we wanted for Christmas because he is magic isn't he! Before I started writing Christmas lists I used to love looking through the Argos magazine and cutting out pictures of what I wanted for Christmas and leave them under my pillow, which Mum used to find when she changed my bedding. I always used to write a Christmas list and give it to Mum to post—hence how she knew what we wanted! I used to hate getting clothes for a present because I wanted toys! Kids, aren't they ungrateful!

With the last few days before Christmas passing and excitement growing, wondering what Santa would bring us and would we have a white Christmas, I used to love walking home from school in the dark and seeing the Christmas tree lights shining from people's house windows. Mum and Dad used to take us for a drive in the evenings to see the Christmas lights, probably making the most of what we could see whilst we could still see! Mum also used to take us into Nottingham for a walk in the evening and show us the Christmas tree lights in the arcade. Now Mum doesn't like to tell me about any Christmas tree lights because she knows it upsets me because I can't see them.

Santa always used to leave our presents in our bedroom at the end of our bed in a pillow case. One year I woke up on Christmas Day to find no presents at the end of my bed. This made me think I had been a naughty girl and I hadn't got any. I then went into Mum's bedroom really upset and said, "Santa hasn't brought me any presents," and Mum said, "Maybe he left them downstairs." I then rushed downstairs and there my presents were. When Alex and I were older Mum told us that she used to have to wait for us to fall asleep before she could creep in with our presents, but one year she decided to leave them downstairs because we didn't settle down to sleep till late.

I still enjoy buying Christmas presents when I am out shopping and then wrapping them up and writing gift tags. I don't like those bags that you can put presents in because I enjoy wrapping presents so much and where's the fun in just putting presents in bags! I don't like receiving presents in those bags either because I enjoy tearing the paper open.

Now it is a lot harder to think what I want for birthdays and Christmas because there isn't much I need and can do because of me being blind. Now it is equally hard to think what to buy Alex as he is blind too. If I get any more CDs or videos I will probably be able to set up my own shop! I prefer to buy things for Mum and Dad that they need like cycling clothes or even get them to buy them so they get the right things and I give them the money.

On Christmas Day Alex and I used to get up really early (6 o'clock time) and creep downstairs to see what we had for Christmas. Mum used to go to midnight mass with her friend Beverly after spending some time at the pub on Christmas Eve, so when Alex and I got up early she wasn't too impressed. The year before I started going to midnight mass I went into Alex on Christmas Day morning at 6.30 and asked if we could get up and Alex said, "No. Go back to bed until 7.00," and I wasn't happy. The year I started going to midnight mass Alex said to me on Christmas Eve, "If you come into me before 7.00 there will be trouble!" and I said, "Yes, and if you come into me before 8.00 there will be trouble!"

After opening our presents we had breakfast which consisted of a mince pie and slice of toast. The rest of the morning was spent cooking dinner and Dad used to make a trifle ready for tea. After dinner we went for a walk to burn some dinner off ready for tea.

Boxing Day we used to spend at my grandma and granddad's house where my aunts and uncles used to converge bringing with them our cousins. At our grandparents' house we always used to have another Christmas dinner on Boxing Day rather than just eating leftovers from the day before. After dinner we used to be really full and my granddad used to say, "Make sure you do plenty for tea because everybody will be hungry!" At tea we used to go and ask granddad what he wanted and the answer always used to be, "Oh just a couple of sausage rolls and a cup of tea," as he wasn't hungry yet everybody apparently would be! After tea we used to watch Songs of Praise when the carol "Once in Royal David's City" used to come on and my granddad would pipe up, "Your Uncle Alban used to sing this in the choir." After a few years of this happening we used to say, "Uncle Alban used to sing this in the choir, didn't he granddad?" and my granddad would say, "How do you know? Have I told you before?" and we used to say, "Yes granddad," in a resigned voice. Another year when the carol came on we looked at granddad as if to say, "Don't say it," and my Aunty Lesley says, "Alban used to sing this in the choir." Alex banged his head on the sofa and my granddad laughed and Aunty Lesley asked, "Have I said something wrong?"

The year before my granddad died he was in hospital in December near Christmas so we went down to his house on Boxing Day. When Mum was doing dinner granddad said, "Don't do much for me because I am not hungry." When granddad saw how much dinner he had got on his plate he said, "Is that it?" and Mum said, "There is more in the oven if you want it." So granddad had extra and he was still first to finish. At tea time Mum went into granddad to see what he wanted, expecting him to say, "A couple of sausage rolls and a cup of tea," but he asked Mum what cobs there were and he had a cob too. Normally granddad doesn't eat trifle, he liked blancmange, but Mum hadn't got any this year, so granddad had some trifle. Mum then came into granddad and asked if anyone wanted seconds and my granddad shook his spoon as if to say yes please. After granddad had eaten his trifle he asked for a mince pie and Mum felt his forehead to see if he was well as he didn't normally eat so much. Mum

6

expected granddad to be more hungry than normal because you don't get much to eat in hospital but not quite that hungry.

Christmas always used to be extra special because of the Boxing Days spent with our grandparents, before they died. After Mum's Mum and Dad died we used to have Boxing Day at home and my other set of grandparents used to come for tea. We used to dismantle the table and take it in the lounge then take all the food through. Dad always makes trifles on the morning of Christmas Day, Boxing Day and New Year's Day ready for tea. We still have a full Christmas dinner on Boxing Day and New Year's Day. Normally on Christmas Eve I help prepare the vegetables for Christmas Day so it is less to do.

Now Christmas isn't quite as special partly because my grandparents are dead and also because I can't see snow when it comes or the Christmas tree lights due to being blind and having to watch what I eat due to being diabetic.

Chapter 2

Growing Up

Alex and I used to get up early at weekends and creep downstairs saying to each other, "Shh, don't wake Mum or Dad up," whilst Mum and Dad used to lie there laughing. Some mornings we used to get up early to watch children's television and there was the test card picture, before 24 hour television came, on making me feel really old. On Sunday mornings after breakfast we watched 'Little House on the Prairie' and 'Rawhide'.

On Saturday mornings we watched 'Power Rangers' and other programmes whilst eating our breakfast in the living room. I used to love Weetabix with milk and sugar on for breakfast. Mum used to put the sugar in a pot for me to put on myself, but I used to be a devil for putting my spoon in the milk before I had put the sugar on and then needing a clean spoon!

Before we had videos of our own to watch I can remember going to a video rental shop to choose videos to borrow. My favourite videos used to be 'Sooty and Sweep', 'Rainbows' and 'Thomas the Tank Engine'. I have a vision of the aircraft coming down and the palm trees falling down in 'Thunderbirds' which I haven't watched for years. The first four Disney videos Mum and Dad bought Alex and I for Christmas were: 'Sleeping Beauty', 'Robin Hood' (animated version), 'Sword in the Stone' and 'Dumbo'. After that we got quite a few videos, some were Disney videos and some were music videos. Alex and I used to watch videos that much that we learned a lot of the words off by heart and we can listen to them even now when we can't see as we know by the music what is happening.

Ever since I learned to talk I have been singing along to Barry Manilow songs from Mum's cassette tapes and CDs and my own Barry Manilow videos. I remember having a Barry Manilow concert that Mum and Dad taped on a video which I used to watch much that it started getting lines through it and Mum had to hide it from me—the trouble was I still used to find it and watch it! From the age of 7 Mum has taken me to Barry

Manilow concerts with her, Aunty Lesley and Beverly. Quite a lot of concerts used to be at the NEC at Birmingham which we got to by a coach from Nottingham which took us to the NEC and waited with us. On the coach they sometimes used to play Barry Manilow music. Some concerts used to be in Nottingham and others further away. We haven't been to one for a long time as they have either been too far away or too expensive, or both.

I then started to listen to Cliff Richard's music which I really liked too. Now I like a lot of music, provided that I can hear what they are singing I will learn the words and sing along. If a song comes on the radio or CD player that I like I can't help singing along to it!

When Alex and I were little Mum got a BBC computer that we used to play games on such as 'Pod', where you could make him fly, run, sink, explode and other things. I also liked puzzle games like 'Palace' and 'Circus' where I had to solve problems or give instructions to get places or objects. Maybe this was what started my interest in solving word puzzles.

Alex and I used to enjoy playing with Duplo and the Duplo Train set as well as playing board games like Ludo. We used to enjoy playing with road mats which we used our toy cars on. Alex used to get annoyed with me as I never got the hang of just driving on one side of the road, but would use both sides! I had a plastic tea set that I used to play with, with my teddy bears.

Alex and I also enjoyed playing with Lego which we could do even when our vision deteriorated as it is tactile—yes there are different colours but what does it matter what colour bricks we used. This idea of not worrying about coloured things also applies to clothes. When I go clothes shopping with Mum I always ask Mum what colour the clothes are that I like but it is the feel and whether they fit me that really matters to me.

Ever since being little I have always enjoyed being crafty (probably in more ways than one) and colouring or painting. I used to love colouring-in books, especially the pictures of flowers and wildlife. Sometimes, if I hadn't got a colouring book but I wanted to colour something in, Mum used to draw round cups and do this lots of times so the circles were overlapping.

Sometimes at the weekend Mum used to let Alex and I paint at the kitchen table using the pallet of six colours and paper/colouring books that she bought from the Early Learning Centre.

Another crafty thing I enjoyed was sticking but I only used Pritt Stick so that the glue didn't go everywhere and make a mess.

When I was really small Mum used to buy plasticine for me to make shapes out of which she used to keep in the fridge.

When Alex and I used to go to the Post Office with Mum we got bottles of blow bubbles to play with.

At home when I wanted to play with a kite in the garden we used to tie wool to plastic bags and use that as a kite but I used to spend a lot of time untangling it from round the wooden clothes line prop and getting splinters.

When I was little I used to spend a lot of time going out for walks with my parents and Alex along our local canal or up town.

I used to like going to the library where I used to borrow books I especially used to like the Theodore Roosevelt books which were about this teddy that used to get up to lots of things. As my vision got worse I spent more time in the library looking for books with larger print.

Sometimes at weekends we used to go to the local park and go on our bikes but once Alex and I got our bikes too close and we both fell off. After this we didn't go on our bikes because it wasn't safe as our sight was starting to deteriorate.

About 20 years ago Dad bought a tandem so he could take us out for rides on it with the Tandem Club or routes that Dad knew. He sometimes used to take me on the tandem to Ambergate where we used to go over the

Milford Tunnel where trains used to go through. When I wasn't tall enough to see over the tunnel wall Dad used to pick me up so I could watch the trains go through.

When Alex and I were old enough to go for walks together, when our sight and hearing wasn't too bad, we used to go for walks to the local Post Office to get cards or up town to the flower shop to get Mum some daffodils, which she really liked.

Dad has always been interested in astronomy so as I grew up I developed an interest in astronomy. Near the top of our garden we have an observatory where we have a telescope and Dad used to show us the planets and stars through it. Sometimes Dad took Alex and I out in the evenings to somewhere where there wasn't as much light pollution and take his small telescope so we could see the planets and stars better. In 1997 Dad told us about a comet that was around which was bright enough to see through binoculars so some nights Dad used to wake us up so we could go outside and see the comet. When Alex and I were trying to grasp the concept of the planets orbiting the sun, Dad used to explain using the salt and pepper pots.

In the evenings or at weekends we used to go out in the car to places like Bradgate Park and Manifold Valley where we used to have a walk. When we were very small we used to go sloe berry or blackberry picking for the wine Mum and Dad used to make. I can't remember anything about the actual wine making but just going to collect the berries.

When we went out in the car we used to occupy ourselves by counting fire hydrants or counting trees that were in blossom. On the way to where we were going on holiday we used to count the touring caravans passing us. I used to love counting the money in my money box where I kept my pocket money, even if I used to know how much would be there just for the pleasure of counting.

I remember wanting Dad to give me piggy backs upstairs so I used to go up a couple of steps so I could climb on his back, and Dad used to play with my toes:

'This little piggy went to market,
This little piggy stayed at home,
This little piggy had all,
This little piggy had none,
And this little piggy said "wee wee wee I'll tell my Mum when she gets home!" '

Before the Council started collecting recycling from our house with the other dustbin rubbish we used to take the bottles to be recycled at the bottle banks. Alex and I really used to enjoy helping Dad with this when we were small. At the bottle banks Dad used to empty one of the crates of bottles so I could stand on it as I wasn't tall enough to reach the hole, and then Dad used to pass me the bottles.

When Alex and I were small and had baths together we used to love playing with the toys in the bath and then we used to go downstairs in front of the gas fire in the winter, and get dry listening to Mum's Disney LP. When we were little we didn't have central heating but just a coal fire. On mornings when it was really cold we used to ask Mum to get the coal fire going quicker than normal. After a few years of this Mum decided to get central heating and now the little man turns it on and warms the house up for us.

It was Dad who first taught me how to swim. On a Saturday morning he used to take Alex and I swimming at our local swimming baths. Dad used to get me to start swimming with his hand helping to hold me up and once I got going he used to move his hand away. I remember going swimming in West Bridgford where my grandparents lived, at Rushcliffe Swimming Baths. On the bottom of the pool there were pictures of monsters that I thought were coming to get me!

In the evenings or at weekends Alex and I used to play football down our entry but I often kicked the ball over the top of the gate and we had to go running down the road to catch the ball. Mum bought Alex and I a skateboard which we used to sit on and go down our road a little. Our balance was not good enough to stand on the skateboard but we didn't mind. We had to stop going on the skateboard when our vision deteriorated so that we didn't bang into the lampposts. We used to love staying in the garden in the summer when it was just starting to get dark and look for bats. Also at weekends I would spend hours lying on a mat in the garden sun bathing and reading my book or doing word searches/crosswords. Once I was outside reading with my magnifier, when Mum went inside to make a cup of tea so I followed, forgetting to take my magnifier in with me. As you can imagine it set the mat on fire but it wasn't anywhere near my book thank goodness!

Once I had a doll called Victoria that I had a push chair for and I used to take her in the push chair together with a wooden dog with wheels on a piece of string for a walk with Mum and Alex. I used to get really angry with the dog because it kept falling over.

Right from being little I have always loved teddy bears which I tie ribbons round to twiddle. I used to take teddy everywhere with me, at home I used to leave him on a chair when I was out or carry him round with me when I was in and I used to throw teddy upstairs before I went upstairs. Once, in summer I had thrown teddy upstairs but I couldn't find him anywhere and it wasn't until Mum went out for something that she found teddy, face down—when I had thrown him upstairs he had gone through the open window! I used to take teddy to my grandparents' house and would worry on the way back home that I had left teddy there and got Mum and Dad to stop to check on the way back home. When I was at nursery I used to take teddy where he would sit on a cupboard so I knew he was there but once I left him there by accident. I then had to borrow a teddy off Mum so I would sleep and then get teddy the next day. I still sleep with my teddy and on occasions when something upsets me I go and sit on my bed and twiddle the ribbon I have round teddy—he is my best friend and like a comfort blanket.

Chapter 3

Holidays

Mum always used to wash teddy ready to take on holiday with us. One year she had packed teddy away in a bag with towels in and I decided I wanted to have a cuddle with him, so I got him out of the bag. It wasn't until we were part way to where we were going on holiday that I panicked because I didn't know where teddy was. Dad pulled over onto the hard shoulder so Mum could have a look in the boot and he wasn't there. Mum had to buy me a teddy so I would sleep. When we got home we found teddy on the table where he had been for 2 weeks whilst we were on holiday.

When I was 8 years old we went on holiday to Hayle in Cornwall and had a really good time. We spent a lot of time playing on the beach building sand castles and swimming or belly boarding in the sea. We either used to have fish and chips from a mobile fish and chip shop or from a pub. I remember going to the pub on site and sitting outside on a bench and watching the sunset—it looked like the sun was sinking into the sea. On the day before we were due to come back home I asked the lady who ran the mobile fish and chip shop if I could stay with her rather than go home, but she said I was best staying with Mum and Dad. The next day I cried all the way home except for when I fell to sleep. When I woke up I asked, "Where are we," and after Mum had said I started crying again because I didn't want to go home, but wanted to be on holiday still.

In 1996 Mum and Dad had finished paying the mortgage and with the left over money we went on holiday to Guernsey. We flew to Guernsey and then hired a car. In Guernsey we stayed in a hotel where we had a family room, me and Alex in a bunk bed and Mum and Dad in the double bed. Whilst we were there we used to go to look around forts, go swimming in the sea and the swimming pool that belonged to the hotel, as well as going on outings to visit the nearby islands. In the evenings we used to go out in the car to look for lighthouses. A couple of times all the power went off in the evenings. The first time this happened the owner of the hotel came out and said, "Hi guys," and we shouted, "Turn the lights on again," thinking it was just a joke. Once we found out it wasn't a joke Dad and I went outside and had a look at the stars.

One day I swam in the sea and then I swam in the pool and had a good time. That evening we had salad and new potatoes for tea which I didn't really like so I didn't have much carbohydrate. That night I had a diabetic fit and Dad had to carry me from the top bunk into bed with Mum so Mum could look after me. After that the owner of the hotel did food for Alex and I that we would eat.

In the year 1999 we went on holiday to a caravan site in Devon for 2 weeks at the same time of year as the solar eclipse. Whilst we were away one of Dad's cycling friends, Jeff Burton, came to stay for a week with us to see the solar eclipse. Although we didn't get the full effect of the eclipse because it was cloudy, it went dark and the birds went quiet. After the eclipse we went for a walk across to the nearby island, Burgh, which you could reach by sand when the tide was out. Whilst we were at the top of a cliff on the island having a rest a lady said, "Look! the sea is coming in and you know how quickly the tide comes in!" and Mum said, "Right, we're going down." When we got to the bottom of the cliff Mum started to undo my trainers and got me to take my socks off as the sea had already come in a bit. We then had to paddle back to the other beach where we dried our feet and put our shoes back on. Now, whenever we ask Dad about his cycling friend called Jeff Burton, we always call him paddling Jeff!

In 2001 we had booked to go on holiday to Felixstowe with my granddad, Aunty Lesley and Aunty Heather for 2 weeks. On the Friday before we went, Mum went up the garden to put the washing out but she was a while so Alex went out to see if she was OK. Alex came back in and told me that Mum had sprained her ankle and was sitting on the grass and I said, "You are joking," and Alex said no. Alex then rang Beverly and told her and she came to help. By the time Beverly got to us Mum had managed to get inside and was kneeling on the floor in floods of tears mopping up the milk that Alex had accidentally knocked on the floor. Beverly then helped Mum up and sorted Alex and I out with our breakfast and then took Mum to hospital, leaving Natalie to be with Alex and I. At hospital they told Mum that she hadn't broken anything but badly sprained it and to go home and sit with her feet up for 48 hours. Mum explained that she couldn't as we were going on holiday the next day and they told her to put her feet up as soon as she got there. On the Friday Alex and I were Mum's gofers whilst she sat on her bed with her feet up whilst she packed the suitcase.

On holiday there were my granddad and Mum who both needed a wheelchair and Alex and I who both needed guiding. Luckily there were 4 people to guide or push us all. To start off my Aunty Heather had to do shuttle service between the seafront and the caravan site as we only had one wheelchair. After a couple of days we got a wheelchair from the local hospital for Mum. After about a week Mum's ankle was still really swollen so she went to the hospital. When she saw the doctor he told Mum she needed to start walking on it and to wash her feet next time before she saw him. Mum is sure he thought the bruises were dirt!

In 2002, the year my granddad died, we had booked to go to Felixstowe. We still went but I remember having to tell the pub landlord about granddad the first night we went to the pub as he wanted to know where he was! We had a good holiday but it wasn't the same without granddad.

Since 2003 we have been going on holiday at least once a year to Holsworthy in Devon. In Holsworthy we stay at Wooda Lakes in a fishing lodge and there are 5 lakes near where we go fishing. When we started going there I wasn't sure if I would like fishing but I caught a fish and that hooked me on fishing. When I first started fishing I learned to do it using a rod with some line tied to it. I have now progressed to using a rod with a reel or using a pole. The biggest carp I have caught these last 13 years was 14 pounds 8 ounces. When Alex and I were little and we could still manage to see the guy ropes of the tent, we used to go on holiday with my Dad's parents to Wales or Caister-on-Sea. In Wales I stayed in a tent with Mum, Dad and Alex and grandma and granddad used to stay in their tent next to us. A couple of nights we stayed in my grandma's tent for a change. Where we stayed was near a beach where Alex and I enjoyed playing. When we were near the tent I used to fly my kite. Once

I let go of my kite by accident and was really upset but Dad went and caught it for me.

I used to like playing in the park on the climbing frames. Once, when I was showing off on a climbing frame where you have to swing from one hoop to another I fell off and landed on my right arm. Mum and Dad took me to the local hospital where I had an X-ray which showed I had sprained it. On the way to the hospital every bump we went over hurt my arm. At the hospital they put my arm in a sling which I had to keep on at night. I found it really hard to push myself up in bed without using that arm, and had to get Alex to help me.

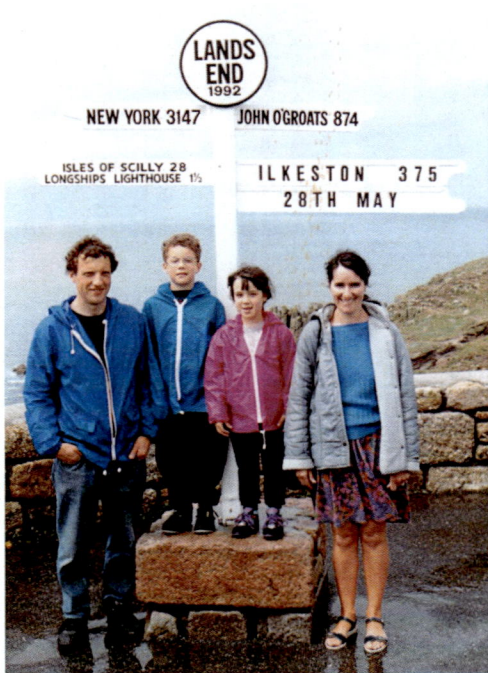

In the 6 weeks holiday I used to go on holiday for 2 weeks with my parents, brother and Mum's parents to Felixstowe where my granddad was born. At Felixstowe we stayed at a caravan site which was right next to a train line and wasn't far from the promenade and beach. As the caravan site was next to the train line Dad used to shout when a train was coming.

Mum used to stick her head out of the kitchen window, whilst grandma poked her head out the back window, and Dad ran out onto the ramp (that we had to help granddad). Once, when an engineer from the caravan site was fitting a rail to the caravan steps, Alex noticed he was fitting it to the wrong side of the steps and told the man, otherwise the door wouldn't close. Another time when dinner was taking ages to cook granddad said, "Come on kids. Let's go across to the club." So we went across and had a packet of crisps to keep us going. When we went back to the caravan my granddad asked my grandma, "Is dinner ready yet?" and my grandma said, "No it isn't," in not a very happy sort of voice. When an engineer came and had a feel of the gas bottle that the cooker was running off he said, "Here is your problem, it's empty." Once he had swapped it to the other bottle we were literally cooking on gas!!

Alex and I spent a lot of time playing on the caravan site in the park or swimming in the pool there or playing on the beach. After going swimming in the pool on site we used to walk back to our caravan, wrapped in our towel and being careful not to stand on a thistle. When Alex and I were little we used to go with granddad for a walk to the beach where granddad used to sit on the breakers whilst Alex and I played in the sand. At the club at the caravan site I used to go to the group they ran for children and take part in activities. In the evenings we used to go to a nearby pub for dinner and I often used to fall asleep on granddad's knee in the wheelchair on the way back to the caravan. Once Mum got my granddad's wheelchair wheels stuck in the railway lines and my grandma said, "Let's leave him there and let him be shunted up to Ipswich!"

Once when I was really small I was jumping over this puddle on the promenade at Felixstowe (like kids do) in front of Mum, Dad, grandma and granddad and Dad said, "Any minute she is going to fall in that puddle," and sure enough I did. My grandma then said, "Right, back to the caravan," where she told me to, "Skin a rabbit," or in other words strip off.

Chapter 4
Family and Friends

Once when Alex and I got home from school we found that Mum had packed some clothes for us all and told us we were going to see grandma and granddad for the weekend. So we set off in the normal direction to grandma's house but when we got to one particular island we went straight on instead of going left which confused us. We then said to Mum, "This isn't the way to grandma's house." A bit later we said to Mum, "We don't know where we are going!"

Mum said to us, "Well, where is grandma?" and we went, "Oh at Felixstowe," and Mum said, "Well then." When we got there it was quite late so we had fish and chips from the fish shop on site. Whenever I mention this to Mum now she will say, "Trust you to remember the food part!"

Dad sometimes used to go away hostelling on his bike for the weekend with some other people, leaving Mum to look after Alex and I. One vivid memory I have of one time he did this was when Mum took things down to my grandparents on the Friday whilst Alex and I were at school. After tea on the Friday we caught the bus to my grandparent's house and I remember walking down Eltham Road (where my grandparents lived) in the twilight when the street lamps were just starting to come on and were a reddish colour. When we got to grandma's house she had a Cliff Richard CD on. Mum and I used to sleep in the big back bedroom together whilst Alex slept in the small back bedroom. On the Saturday evening we walked to the Willow Tree pub where we had tea with my grandparents, when we were walking back grandma remarked that she could smell rain and a storm on the way. Sure enough when we got back it threw it down with rain and on the Sunday morning we had a thunderstorm.

One particular day in May when I was only 4 Mum told Alex and I that our cousin Nikki was coming for the day. When Nikki got to our house her Dad (our Uncle Tony) got out with her suitcase so that told us straight

21

away that she had come for more than a day. Whilst Nikki stayed she taught Alex and I how to use the children's computer that we hadn't played with much until then. One hot day we all went to Ladybower Dam where Alex and I were playing with sticks in the water like kids do. Luckily Mum had stripped me down to pants and socks and shoes because once my foot slipped and I got wet.

We spent a lot of time at my grandparent's house in West Bridgford. Luckily for Alex and I, both sets of grandparents lived next door to each other so we could see both sets at the same time. Ideal! It was my grandma who set me off counting things especially the cherry stones we used to find in cherry pies—we used to have a competition to see who could find the most in their piece of pudding. It was grandma who taught me how to do word search puzzles and sometimes I used to do puzzles out of her book. Once I was doing a puzzle with the letter q in all the words and I asked grandma, "What does anti-que and uni-que mean?" When I first saw the words and I didn't know how to say them I did what they tell you—break it up into syllables.

As children Alex and I used to enjoy crawling under my grandma's settee with her draft excluders which were shaped like snakes. I also crawled under the table when I wanted to get out from my seat. My grandma Maggie had a bush (cotoneaster) in front of her bay window that had berries on it and I used to spend a lot of time on my hands and knees sweeping up the berries. When Alex and I were little our grandma Maggie had an apple tree. When the apples were ready to be picked grandma used to knock the branches with her walking stick whilst Alex and I ran around catching the apples. Alex and I loved going ladybird catching with Mum or our Aunty Lesley along my grandma's road. We also loved going for walks along the canal which ran at the end of the road. In my grandma's garden she had a foxglove plant which I used to love poking my fingers into the glove like flowers—doesn't bear thinking about now but I never used to worry about bees being inside the flowers then.

Sometimes down at my grandma's house Mum used to take me to my Aunty Heather's house where I used to play battleships with my cousin James. When my cousins Wesley and Gregory were at my grandma's house they used to do 'a leg and a wing to see the king with a one, two and a jolly good three' with Alex and I. When my cousin Nikki was at grandmas with us we used to play doctors and nurses in my grandma's big back bedroom.

Whilst we were down at my grandparents' house Mum used to look after the garden cutting the grass and bushes when they needed cutting. On my granddad's lawn he had ornaments which I used to move for Mum so she could mow the lawn. Once I was clearing the ornaments and I asked, "What is this log doing here," and Mum replied, "It is a wooden squirrel." Once Mum was trimming bushes with the secateurs and she was going to come the next day to do some more but the secateurs needed sharpening so Alex went into granddad and said, "Granddad, can you sharpen the secateurs for Mum ready for tomorrow because she is going to come back and do some more," and granddad said, "Oh dear." Another time Mum was doing bits in the garden and granddad stood at the window shaking his head as he saw his garden disappearing in front of his eyes. Once when my grandma and granddad were on holiday Mum thought right I will cut some bushes whilst they aren't here. When granddad got back he asked Mum, "Have you been in my garden?" and Mum told him that yes she had as he knew and she named a few things she had done at granddad's, "And the rest!" he said.

Every other Sunday grandma and granddad used to come to our house for the day to save us from going to their house all the time. In the morning granddad used to go for a walk on his two crutches whilst I played with my tea set and my teddies at home with grandma and Alex.

Mum and Dad weren't born next to each other, Dad was born down the Meadows and Mum was born in West Bridgford. In 1971 Dad and his brother and parents had to move house and it just so happened that they bought the house next to Mum and her parents. Mum and Dad started going out in 1972 and they got married in 1975. Unfortunately Mum and Dad hadn't found a house to live in by then so they had to live with Mum's parents for 6 months before they found the house in Ilkeston.

I still live in Ilkeston where I was born, with my Mum, Dad and older brother Alex, who is 2 years older than me.   My bedroom where I am writing this story is bigger than it used to be because we had my bedroom and Alex's extended in 1997 as well as the lounge.   We had this extension to give Alex and I more room to do things in our bedroom so Mum and Dad could spend time in the lounge together.

Ever since Alex and I were little we have always got on really well and liked playing together with teddies or watching telly or videos together. Even when we haven't got on we have never fallen out or fought.   When Alex and I were little we sometimes wished we hadn't got a sibling and my Dad's Dad (our granddad) used to tell us how lucky we were to have a sister/brother as he was an only child.

I am very close to my Mum and love giving her cuddles and kisses even when she is doing something.   If Mum is washing the pots whilst I am in the kitchen with her I will creep up behind her and give her a cuddle— because of this Mum calls me Barnie short for barnacle since I am always cuddling her.   When I go out for a meal with Mum and my carer I prefer to hold onto Mum and whilst we are sitting at the table waiting in the restaurant I will hold Mum's hand.   I don't get to spend as much time with

Dad as I do with Mum as Dad works Monday to Friday at Raleigh so I only see him in the evenings and at weekends, whereas Mum doesn't work because she is a full-time carer for Alex and I. The only other time Dad has off is at Christmas or when we go on holiday but it takes him a few days to get used to being around Alex and I. The time I do spend with Dad I really enjoy especially when we hold hands or have a cuddle and kiss. Even now I still give Mum and Dad a cuddle and kiss before I go to bed.

Mum finished school in 1971 and started working at Lady Bay Cleaners where she worked for a couple of years before she left there and got a job at Jessops. Mum then worked at Jessops up until she had Alex and she intended to go back to work when I was 5 years old. Mum was 12 weeks pregnant with Alex before she knew, so it came as a surprise for Mum. One test Mum had when she was pregnant with Alex showed that there might be an abnormal birth i.e. she might have twins (this was possible as Mum was a twin) but Alex was born normally. Alex was born 2 weeks early which looking back isn't a surprise as he hasn't got much patience.

When Mum was pregnant with me she thought at one point that I was stuck but the doctor told her that I wasn't. I was born 2 weeks late—well I am very close to Mum so I probably didn't want to come out but wanted to stay close to Mum. I used to lie with my back against Mum's stomach so her tummy was rock hard. The morning I was born was when Mum should have been induced. When Mum told them at hospital that she didn't need to be induced they sent her to a suite and told her that her second baby would be ages yet. When Mum had called the ladies through after a few hours they were surprised that she wanted to push already. As it turns out I had got stuck as I had the cord wrapped round my neck twice. For the first 6 weeks I slept all day and cried all night until Mum got my clock changed round. Mum says Alex was the baby from heaven and I was the baby from hell, if Mum could have sent me back she would have. But now it is the other way round.

Alex and I have always been very close. Alex wouldn't have anything to do with me when I was a baby until I started walking and talking but he loved sterilising my things for me. When I started walking and talking

Alex used to say to Mum, "I will occupy Keri for you," which he did. Alex loved feeding me at meal times and I remember saying, "Feed me, feed me Alex," one time. Mum has got a photo somewhere of Alex feeding me spaghetti whilst I sat in a high chair. Alex and I spent a lot of time together when we were little and we could always talk to each other about our condition and support each other.

I am closer to Mum than Dad only because we spend more time together because of Dad being at work 5 days a week and cycling a lot but I still really get on well with Dad too. Dad and I don't cuddle quite as much as I do with Mum but when we do cuddle I really enjoy it. Dad is very practical about the best way for me to do things, like when I couldn't see where to put the blood on the testing strip, Dad drew a black arrow on a margarine tub lid and cut it out so I could line it up with the strip.

Dad has got one brother called Guiliano (my uncle) who Alex and I used to either call "Uncle Junk" or just "Uncle". My uncle lived at his parents (my grandparents) house for many years and when we were down there we spent a lot of time together playing dominoes or cards. He taught me how to play a domino game called fives and threes where if the number on each end of the line of dominoes on the table was in the 3 or 5 times table you scored points. We played a card game called 7 card brag which we used to play quite a lot. When Alex and I were quite small uncle tried teaching us how to play chess and draughts, I understand draughts but I can't get my head round chess very well. Once my uncle said to me, "You're my best niece, you are," and I replied straight away, "I am the only one you've got!" And he said, "Oh aye," as he didn't expect me to say it straight away.

Mum has got 3 brothers and 3 sisters and they used to use my grandparents' house as a gathering point when they were alive. As they don't have this anymore we all meet up once or twice a year sometimes to celebrate things but we meet up every year anyway. When we meet up we go and have dinner together at a pub in West Bridgford where there are about 16 of us altogether.

My Aunty Marian (my Mum's sister) lives in Norfolk now, but when she lived in Awsworth Alex and I used to see her quite regularly at my house where she used to come for a chat, sometimes bringing with her, her first dog Ozzy which Alex and I played with outside with his toys. Aunty Marian came down to our grandparents' house quite a lot, just dropping in when she had time. Whilst in Awsworth Aunty Marian had a job at a local primary school which unknown to us at the time was where my friend Shirley Cole used to work so she had heard about Alex and I for years before we met. Aunty Marian got Alex and I a lot of A3 rolls of paper that we used to enjoy drawing maps on. When Alex and I stopped playing with toys that were suitable we used to give them to Aunty Marian to take to the nursery where she worked with the children. In return the children used to do large print thank you cards. Now Alex and I enjoy going down to see my Aunty Marian in Norfolk with Mum and a carer to spend the day there.

Ever since I was little I have always loved helping in the house wherever I can. Once when I was about 7 years old I was drying the pots for Mum, I accidentally dropped a plate on my foot sideways on and it broke my big toenail. I remember having to wear boots to school for a couple of days whilst my toe got better instead of my school shoes. Once when I was drying the pots I thought "Wow that is a big bubble" and started trying to blow it out and Mum asked what I was doing. It turned out to be a Pyrex bowl. Since then the Pyrex bowl has been known as the glass bubble! I also enjoy helping to prepare vegetables; peel carrots, potatoes and parsnips, chop cabbage, mix Yorkshire puddings. I love to cook and mix recipes. I help straighten washing and put it on radiator airers and then keep checking to see if it is dry and fold it. When my vision was better I used to do ironing for Mum—only the flat things like underwear, t-shirts and bedding. Somebody once showed me how to iron shirts and trousers but I could never get my head round it with all the creases and seams.

* * *

When Mum was pregnant with me and she was getting a double pushchair she met up with Beverly, who she has been friends with ever since. Beverly who used to live a few minutes away has two children called

Matthew and Natalie, who are about the same age as me, who I used to play with.

I used to spend a lot of time playing with Matthew and Natalie at their house, playing board games or watching videos, or in their back garden on my bike. We sometimes used to have tea at Beverly's house and one particular day Beverly was asking Mum if she should do (R I C E) and I said, "Oh, I would like rice please."—Mum said then she should have known I was going to be clever! We used to go to Wollaton Park or Bramcote Park where we either played football or threw frisbees. When we used to go to the cinema together to see a film, we used to have dinner out nearby and then after the film we used to walk home calling in at the chip shop for a cone of chips.

Chapter 5

Infant School

Matthew and Natalie went to the same school as Alex and I which was a ten minute walk from my house. On mornings when Beverly had to start work early, she dropped Matthew and Natalie off at my house and Mum used to take us all up to school.

At infant school I used to bring a reading book home, read it that night to Mum and get another book the next day—I was a book worm! I used to then ask Alex if I could read his book to which I used to get a "no" in response, but Mum used to sneak the book to me in secret. By the time I was in Alex's year I had read all of his books so they had to find something different for me to read.

Mum used to come and listen to readers at my school, so whenever my teacher announced that Mrs Chambers was listening to readers, I used to think, "Oh good, Mum is here!" Once my teacher even sent me to read to Mum, and Mum thought, "Oh no, I listen to her at home!"

One word I struggled with was the word sausage, as it is a funny spelling—shouldn't it be spelt 'sosage'? To start off with, every time I came across the word Mum had to tell me many times what it spelt before I got it.

When I was in the reception class I did the mental arithmetic test with the other children, where I got top marks. My teacher Mrs Monk told Mum later, that she could see me wriggling my fingers and toes, whilst I was doing the test. A standing joke at home is that I was OK as long as the number didn't get any bigger than 20, otherwise I would run out of fingers and toes! Mrs Monk told Mum that I didn't need to do the rest of infant's school, but just to send me straight to junior school, but I still completed the rest of infant's school like everybody else.

In the first year, I used to stay behind after school with some other children and learn how to play the recorder. When I used to practise at home, Mum used to send me up the garden—was my recorder playing that bad!

In my final year of infant's school, my teacher was called Mrs Tucker, who later told Mum, that I never used to be afraid of telling other children to behave if they were being naughty. Apparently I used to come home and tell Mum whose names had been on the blackboard.

In my last year a lady came in and taught us a little French and she taught us the song Frere Jacques.

At infant school I used to play games with the other children, like What Time Is It Mr Wolf? We played a game where two people faced each other and made a bridge with their arms, through which someone else used to go, whilst they sang 'orange and lemon said the bells of saint Clement'. Two songs we were taught at school were 'Let's Go Fly A Kite' out of Mary Poppins and 'We All Live In A Yellow Submarine'. I really used to like the two harvest festival songs we sang:

See the fields so bare and brown,
Feel the nights turn cold,
Lamps are early lit in town,
Hunter's moon shines gold.

Thank you Lord for rest and food,
For the harvest safely stored,
Sing a thankful song of praise,
Autumn time this year.

Cauliflowers fluffy and cabbages green,
Strawberries sweeter than any I've seen,
Beetroot purple and lettuces flat,
Radishes round and runner beans fat.

The apples are ripe,
The plums are red,
Broad beans are sleeping,
In their blankety bed.

There is more of that one but I can't remember all the words.

We used to have a Sports day each year, and when I was in my last year, I competed in the wheelbarrow race with another girl—I was the one leaning on my arms whilst the other girl held my legs. Alex and I used to practise doing this up the garden on the grass.

Mum used to help out when we went on school trips, and there were three boys in my year that never did as they were told, and used to end up holding Mum's hand because they couldn't be trusted, which they didn't used to like. Whichever one was holding Mum's hand used to say, "Why do I always have to hold your hand?" and Mum used to say, "Because you don't do as you're told!" They used to reply, "I will be good," and Mum used to say, "Well prove it," and sure enough they used to end up holding Mum's hand again.

My infant school is still there under the same headmistress, but it has changed a lot, having had extensions to make more classrooms. Most of my school teachers have now retired.

Right from being in the Nursery Mum had to send biscuits and sugar-free drinks for Alex and I to have at break time, since we were both diagnosed diabetic by then. Once I remember sitting in assembly one morning and going hypo, and waking up in the staff room at break time, eating biscuits.

Chapter 6
How it all Started

As far back as I can remember, I have always seen Alex injecting himself, but I never used to think anything of it—I just thought it was part of growing up! Okay, I didn't used to see Mum or Dad injecting themselves, but maybe they did it in private or maybe you just did it up to a certain age. It wasn't until I started having to inject, and I wasn't allowed sweet food, that I found out I had diabetes the same as Alex, hence the injections.

When I was about 4 years old I went down with chickenpox, which triggered the diabetes. I used to go to Nursery fine but when Mum came to pick me up and we started walking home I started to complain of hunger pangs, so Mum had to carry me back home. I then started drinking, going to the toilet a lot and being in a bad mood, all of which Mum had seen before because Alex had been diagnosed diabetic 3 years previously. Mum recognised the symptoms and tested my blood sugars and ketones using Alex's kit, which proved that I was diabetic, so on my doctor's notes it says "diagnosed by Mum". Luckily for me, Mum recognised the symptoms so I was able to start doing injections before the diabetes made me ill—unlike Alex. Doing injections never used to bother me as I had seen Alex doing injections for so long. To start off with I didn't understand why I couldn't have sugary food but as I grew I learned more about diabetes. When I was diagnosed diabetic it really upset Mum—it had been hard enough with Alex being diabetic, but now having two with diabetes and Mum worried about me having diabetes and wanting children of my own. After a time Mum got used to us being diabetic and didn't think two children with just diabetes was too bad!

When we were first diagnosed diabetic we started on 2 injections a day and because of this we had to follow a strict regime. We had to have breakfast no later than 8.00am and a portion of 30 grams of carbohydrate, at break time we had to have a biscuit or something else to keep us going until dinner. We had to have dinner about 12.00pm consisting of a portion of food which was 40 grams in carbohydrate. About 5.00pm we had tea consisting of 50 grams of carbohydrate. From this you can tell we had to check how much carbohydrate was in food and make sure it wasn't too sweet. The first few times Mum went shopping after I had been diagnosed it took her ages as she had to check the labels on food wrappers. We could only have a pudding once a week as a treat and only a small portion.

Once at my grandma's house I needed a biscuit for my snack so I had a look at what biscuits she had got open. I then asked grandma, "How much do you think these are?" and grandma said she didn't know so I said, "Well I better have two just to be on the safe side!" When Mum heard she said one probably would have been enough. Dad said, "That is it, eat first ask questions later," and that is my motto now.

When Alex was first diagnosed diabetic the doctors only told Mum that he would need injections for the rest of his life, he never told us that we could have diabetic fits. When I was about 4 years old I remember waking up because Alex was shouting so I went into Mum and told her. Mum went into Alex and tried giving him a cuddle thinking he was having a bad dream but he kept pushing Mum away so she eventually rang the doctors. Whilst Mum was waiting for the doctors she tried taking Alex to the toilet with Dad's help but Alex had lost the feeling down the left side of his body. When the doctor came he tried running his keys down Alex's foot but his left foot didn't move at all compared to his right foot. Mum asked the doctor if he wanted a drink but the doctor said that we needed to take Alex straight to hospital which we did. Mum had to take me to hospital too since I hadn't long been diagnosed diabetic so we stayed over with Alex until his blood sugars got better.

I have had several diabetic fits in the past—the first one really scared Mum as my eyes rolled into the top of my head and I went completely still and Mum thought I was dead. Mum rang for an ambulance straight away and when they came they wanted a doctor to come so Mum rang them and explained what had happened. After about 10 minutes no doctor appeared so the ambulance driver rang and the doctors said as it was my first diabetic fit to take me straight to hospital. The ambulance driver told Mum they would have to take me to QMC because that was where they took people. Mum explained that all my notes were at City Hospital so she rang the Papplewick ward but they said they couldn't take me there. By this point I had had one diabetic fit at home. When I got to hospital the doctors were just setting everything out ready to do my blood sugars and things when I had another fit so everything went to the four corners of the room. The junior doctor then asked Mum if I liked needles and when Mum asked why they explained that they needed to give me glucose and Mum just told them to do it—what did it matter if I liked needles or not! When they tried putting a cannula in my hand to give me the glucose I kept trying to pick it out because I wasn't fully with it, so they had to strap my hand to a board so I couldn't get to it. At about 2 in the morning they decided to transfer me to City Hospital in an ambulance but a nurse had to come with us in case I had another fit. When I got to the ward they got me settled and Mum went to have a shower but as soon as Mum had gone I woke up wanting to know where Mum was, so I went and sat with the nurses. It was typical that I woke up as soon as Mum had left me, like a light bulb had been switched on as soon as Mum left me.

When I went to my next Diabetic clinic appointment Mum told the consultant about the fit and about City Hospital saying they couldn't take me straight away, so the consultant gave Mum a pink admissions card that Mum needed to show the ambulance driver, stating that I needed to go straight to the City Hospital. Alex and I have had several diabetic fits since then on the insulin we were on as it stayed in our system too long rather than just using the sugar up from our meal.

Since then the Diabetes consultant has changed the insulin to another type so I haven't had as many fits—thank goodness. Most of the fits I have had have been during the night so I haven't known much about them but I have had a few in the day which have really scared me. One time when we were on holiday, I had a fit when I was awake when we were walking down a canal towpath and we hadn't got any lucozade or sugary drink with us. Luckily I had a few sugary things with me but it took a long time for my blood sugars to come up. Once I had stopped fitting Dad managed to get me a ride in a canoe back to the car so I wouldn't have to walk, since we didn't want my blood sugars to drop again. When we were back at the place we were staying Mum did my blood sugars and it was sky high which we weren't surprised about after all the sugar I had had.

When I was about 12 years old I changed from doing 2 injections a day to 4 injections a day which made controlling the diabetes much easier and I didn't have to be so strict with meal times and how much I could eat.

As a result of having diabetes Alex and I had to go to get our eyes checked at the hospital twice a year to make sure there wasn't any sign of retinopathy. When our vision started to deteriorate and we went to our hospital clinic with the consultant we were diagnosed with Optic Atrophy. It was really hard for Alex and I losing our sight, due to the colour blindness we got red and green mixed up, pink and grey and purple and blue which was really frustrating. We could never read the print in greeting cards due to it being fancy writing—why can't they just use normal Ariel type writing instead of using fancy writing all the time. Whenever Alex or I needed to buy a greeting card we had to get somebody to read them to us. Luckily the post master at our local Post Office was very helpful and used to help us rather than Mum having to read the card to us that was for her!

We stopped being able to play out on our bikes because we had lost our peripheral sight.

Even after Alex and I were diagnosed diabetic and started on injections we still used to get up to go to the toilet a lot during the night. Mum thought it was just us—like a lot of things that we found out these were due to the medical condition with which we were later diagnosed. Mum and Dad used to take a glass of water to bed with them and bring me and Alex a cup of water. They always used to call me "the secret water drinker" because if I was thirsty during the night I used to drink my water first, and then if I was still thirsty drink Alex's water and then if I was still thirsty I used to drink Mum's. After a while Mum started taking a bottle of water upstairs so that if I drank my water I could fill it up from the bottle. Unfortunately I can't do that now and have to try and save my water as I am on a restricted fluid allowance.

Before Alex and I were diagnosed with Diabetes Insipidus we never used to want to eat much because we drank a lot. To get us to eat Mum used to tell us that there were people waiting for us to eat something and she had to invent all these imaginary people. Now when I am hungry and my tummy is rumbling, I think of men sitting at a table banging their cutlery on the table, or men going through the cupboards trying to find something to eat.

Ever since being little I have always suffered with my hearing and apparently I failed my hearing test when I was a baby but this was put down to selective hearing and distractions. Mum always found that my speech was never as clear as Alex's but she never used to think anything of it, as you get used to your child's voice don't you! Once my grandma mentioned my speech to Mum and said Mum ought to get it checked and got me in for a hearing test, where I was diagnosed with a mild hearing loss. It wasn't until I was in the second year junior that I had to start wearing hearing aids. To start with I wouldn't wear them but if I used to ask Alex to repeat what he just said he would say, "Well I am not telling you again." After Alex had been saying this for a while I started to wear my hearing aids.

When I was 16 I was transferred from children services to adult services. Mum found out that I had a severe hearing loss and I used to need radio aids to help me hear at school. Now I have got profound hearing loss in my right ear and severe hearing loss in my left ear. The hearing aids I have got are the strongest ones on the market and they are turned up as loud as they go, so if my hearing gets worse there isn't anything they can do to help me.

I find it really frustrating when I can't hear what people are saying especially if it is noisy. I used to like listening to Countdown on telly but I don't watch this anymore as I get frustrated when I find out I have made words with letters that weren't there because I misheard. I have a lot of difficulty understanding people on the telephone especially if they have an accent or a really soft voice. People suggest that we get a text phone which would be great if I could see it! Once we got a letter from our local Council about sending me for lip reading classes, what am I supposed to do, feel the person's lips all the time!

When Alex and I were little we both had a child's bike each which we used to ride along our entry. I always struggled to balance on the bike and had to lean against the wall to stop me falling off. It wasn't until Dad took my bike to Wollaton Park and got me to ride my bike without stabilisers down a grassy slope that I got the hang of it. It was a good idea of Dad's for me to practise riding down a grassy slope then if I did fall off I wouldn't hurt myself too much. Mum always used to think I was clumsy when I was little because I always used to fall over grazing my knees. Due to this Mum used to dress me in thick tights or trousers then if I did fall over it would rip my clothes not my skin.

Thinking back now I remember near the end of infant school not being able to see who was on the field as soon as I went out to play. I never thought anything of this as if you can't see something you just get closer don't you!

The ophthalmologist wondered if the diabetes and optic atrophy were related so he referred Alex and I to go and see a neurologist. When Alex and I saw the neurologist he explained that there was a condition which included diabetes and optic atrophy so he sent me and Alex to have some tests done. The neurologist then asked Mum a lot of questions to see if we had any other symptoms relating to this condition. After the neurologist had finished asking Mum the questions Mum didn't need to wait for the results of the tests as we had nearly ticked all the boxes. We then spent an away day at the QMC with Mum and her friend Beverly where we had a kidney scan, hearing test and a CT scan plus a blood test which confirmed that we had Didmoad syndrome.

Didmoad is an acronym for Diabetes Insipidus (water diabetes), Diabetes Mellitus (sugar diabetes), Optic Atrophy and Deafness. These are the main components of the condition but there are other symptoms which present themselves; Alex and I have both got Chronic Lethargy Fatigue Syndrome and lowered immunity.

It seems like we spent a lot of time either at the doctors or local hospital when we were little with one thing or another. In the evenings when we had to go to our local hospital due to one of us having a trapped nail or something we used to tidy up the games in the children's play area. I still have a lot of hospital appointments to go to where I enjoy doing crosswords with Mum to pass the time.

Alex and I were eventually diagnosed with the condition called Didmoad Syndrome in October 1992. Mum was told that we would both go blind and deaf and have a shorter life expectancy. When Mum found out about the shorter life expectancy it really upset Mum and Dad, but luckily they didn't tell us until we were older. At first Mum worried constantly how much time she would get to spend with us, but then she realised she was best just making the most of the time she had with us, rather than worrying about it.

Mum and Dad always used to tell us to grab any chances that came our way with both hands and do what we could whilst we could still do it.

When Alex's and my vision deteriorated to the point where we couldn't see to ride our bikes, Mum and Dad bought a tandem, so Dad could take us out on it. Once when Dad was taking either me or Alex on the tandem Mum said, "You won't get me on that contraption!" Now we can't get her off the tandem but we don't mind as we can't go on the tandem anymore because of our balance being poor.

We used to go camping at the York Cycle Rally for the weekend with Mum and Dad and we used to take the tandem with us. On the Saturday Dad used to take Alex on the tandem with the other people doing this cycle ride whilst Mum and I spent time near the tent. On the Sunday we all went to York Minster to the service and then Dad took me on the tandem on the ride that was organised whilst Mum and Alex walked back from the Minster to the camp site.

When Alex and I started losing our sight and we started tripping over the guy ropes of the tents, Mum used to tie plastic bags to them so we could see them better. This helped us to a certain point but you can't go round tying plastic bags to everybody's tent's guy ropes can you!

Alex and I were traumatised when we first found out about the condition and that we would both go deaf and blind. Apparently I said to Mum once, "When my sight gets better can I ride my bike like that girl," and Mum had to explain that my sight wouldn't get better which upset me. I used to get upset about the condition and the limitations I had especially when I was a teenager with my hormones going haywire so Mum suggested that I take a supplement called Oil of Evening Primrose which I think helped me with my emotions. When Alex and I were diagnosed with the condition Mum and Dad weren't offered any support or told about any families who had children with the condition who she could talk to. Mum ended up writing a letter to the Balance magazine (the diabetic magazine) asking if there were any families out there who had children with the condition or knew about the condition to contact us. Mum eventually got some replies to the letter by post or phone. One of the ladies, who Mum heard from, called Sue, had a son with the condition and she met up with Mum, Alex and I for many years to talk about things. Mum also heard from a family down in Essex who had two children with the condition. When we were on holiday at Felixstowe we sometimes used to go and visit them. Mum is now the contact parent for Contact a Family for families to contact about the condition, if they need to. When we go down to Devon we meet up with Katie who has the condition to exchange news.

Growing up with the condition wasn't easy, having to go through education the same as everybody else whilst our medical condition deteriorated. In some ways we had extra things to learn like Braille and touch typing because we couldn't see.

I remember sometimes at grandma's house she used to ask me and Alex what was the matter and we used to say, "We are fed up," and she used to reply, "Fed up at your age, there must be something wrong with you," and we used to say, "There is!" Alex and I used to receive counselling from different people over the years so that we could talk things through, some used to be friends and others were medically trained in counselling.

Chapter 7
Special Holidays

When Alex and I hadn't long been diagnosed with the condition, we went to a couple of Sense weekends with Mum. At these weekends Mum used to go off with the other parents to do workshops, whilst Alex and I both had a carer to keep us occupied. We were supported by the carer all day and then after our tea that we had with the other children with sense problems we went into a room where we watched videos. Mum and the other parents then had their tea and then would come to collect us ready for bed. Some of the children used to fall asleep before their parents came for them, but I refused to go to sleep before I had seen Mum!

When Alex and I were in the Paediatrics Diabetic clinic they used to take children out for holidays over the weekend. When Alex was 10 he got the chance to go away to Haversage with other children with diabetes for the weekend. Mum and Dad asked if they could take me too so it was a holiday for them too. On the Friday evening we went for a walk nearby in the woods and by the time we got back to where we stayed, Alex was having a fit and spent all night downstairs with the Diabetic liaison, who kept an eye on Alex's blood sugars. On the Saturday we went for a walk over Stanage Edge. On the Sunday we went to Ladybower Dam where we hired bikes to ride round the dam. As there was both Alex and I who needed to ride a tandem and there was only one tandem to hire, Mum and Dad took our tandem for one of us to ride.

The following year when I was 10 I got the chance to go to Haversage and Alex came too, and we did the same sort of activities and yes Alex had a diabetic fit on the Friday evening again!

Alex and I went away on a holiday for diabetics for a week when we were about 12, not far from home in Derbyshire. Whilst we were away we went swimming quite a lot and took part in other activities. I remember having to queue before each meal to see the Diabetic liaison with the other children and sleeping in dormitories. When we were away it gave Mum and Dad a break. Then the year after we went on a 2 week holiday for diabetics in King's Lynn. During this holiday we went roller skating twice amongst other activities. One activity we did was set in a wooded area where we all had a life and it was one group against another trying to steal each other's life. In the evenings the rest of the children watched videos whilst Alex and I went to play snooker. For this holiday Mum sent our nose sprays for the Diabetes Insipidus in a cool pack which then had to be kept in the fridge, but instead of keeping these in the fridge they kept them in the cool box, which meant by the time a few days had gone by they didn't work properly and I was up and down to the toilet a lot at night. I once caught the staff pretending to be ghosts at night whilst I was up going to the toilet. During the last week Alex decided he didn't want to stay any longer. He wanted grandma and granddad to come and fetch us. But I told him that if he went I would go too, but he eventually decided to stay.

Whilst we were away Mum and Dad went for a camping holiday in Norfolk nearby and they kept sending us post cards.

When Alex was 15 he went with the Diabetic clinic with other diabetic children, on a barge trip over the weekend. The following year I went on the barge trip and I had a go at steering the barge and opening and closing a lock with another girl. I wanted to open/close the lock but I found it very unnerving being so close to the water.

When I was 17 I got the chance to go away with the Diabetic clinic to the Hartington youth hostel, with another diabetic girl, who acted as my support person for the weekend. Whilst we were away we were divided into groups where each group took turns in cooking everybody else meals and got awarded on how good it was for diabetics.

As a result of us having a shorter life expectancy, Mum arranged for us to go and see Santa with the charity "Wish Upon A Star", which Alex and I knew nothing about until the morning we were going. On the morning we were going Dad came to wake me up and told me I was going to Lapland to see Santa. I didn't believe him, as he used to wind me up a lot about not going on holiday when we had the car packed ready saying it was just a rehearsal. Mum had to come and wake me up after Dad had told her that I wouldn't believe him and Mum said, "Oh, I wonder why that is!" Dad then took us to East Midlands airport where we were flying from, but unfortunately only one adult could go with us even though there were two of us. This was the first time Alex and I had flown so when we were flying along the runway, Alex asked Mum why we had to go so fast and Mum was just saying, "We have to go so fast so we can take off," when we left the ground. At one point during the flight I said to Mum, "I don't think we are moving," and Mum said, "I hope we are!"

Later in the flight I was looking out the window and I said to Mum, "Look at all that snow down there," and Mum said, "It's not snow its clouds," and I said, "Well it looks like snow to me!"

When we got to Lapland we were very warm as the temperature was 6 Celsius and we were wearing clothes for temperatures of -14 Celsius. When Mum was buying us thermal gloves, balaclavas and snow boots, we wanted to know why and Mum said, "Oh it's going to be really cold this year!" In Lapland the ice was so thick that they even had bonfires on the ice. At one point a man said to Mum, "Look at that crack." Mum said, "Don't talk to me about cracks."

At a restaurant where we had dinner, they had what appeared to me, to be weird food that they eat in Lapland. Alex and I wanted to know if there were chips to eat and Mum said, "They won't have chips in Lapland." A waitress came and said, "Chips for the children," and Mum sighed in relief.

We then went for a sleigh ride pulled by reindeer to see Santa and the man in charge of the sleigh said, "We shall put your Mum at the back because it doesn't matter if she falls off," jokingly.

On the way back home Mum and I felt travel sick, so when the food came round we sent ours away but Alex had his. Alex was just finishing his when I decided I wanted a little bit.

Mum was so tired when she was going through the metal detectors at the airport that she forgot about the metal bell we had bought from Lapland.

Dad was waiting for us when we got to the airport to take us home. In the car on the way home Alex and I fell asleep so when we got home Mum and Dad had to carry us up to bed and undress us whilst we were sleeping.

The next time I went to my grandma's house I said to grandma, "Santa wears glasses."

Grandma straight off the cuff said, "I should think so with all the letters he has to read!"

Alex and I also got the chance to go to Florida with the charity "Dream Flight" when I was 10 years old. The day we went Mum and Dad took us down to the Heathrow hotel next to the airport where we stayed that night, after having a party which comedians came to. On the aeroplane we went over Cape Canaveral. In Florida we stayed in a hotel in Orlando from which we went to Disneyland, MGM Studios and Sea World. I remember feeding the stingrays and dolphins whilst we were there and watching a play. In Disneyland I enjoyed going on the rides Space Mountain, Thunder Mountain and Splash Mountain. Splash Mountain was and is the only log flume I will go on! On the last day we were in Orlando we had a tornado which cracked one corner of the hotel, so a crane had to hold the hotel up. Luckily we were able to take off to fly back home the following day. I remember going outside after the tornado and it was like a hot bath was pouring over me. When we flew back home I didn't get to sleep until midnight and our doctor came to wake us up at 2.00am for our breakfast, because of the 5 hour time difference. When I got home Mum started doing some ironing and she asked me to go upstairs and fetch some coat hangers for her, but I took longer than she expected. Mum ended up coming upstairs to see where I had got to and found me fast asleep on my bed sitting up still holding the coat hangers.

Chapter 8

Junior School

When I left infant's school I went straight up to Markeaton primary school in Derby where Alex was. This school had a visually impaired unit attached to the mainstream school so they could provide us with large print work or magnifiers to help us when we needed them, rather than having to wait for them to be ordered in, like Alex had to at the junior school near where we live.

During Alex's time at an earlier primary school he had been made fun of by the other children because he couldn't see very well and found it difficult to write anything down. To others Alex's writing appeared as a set of squiggles. As a consequence of this Alex lost all confidence. The school had tried to get the resources that Alex needed, but by the time it came Alex's sight had deteriorated even more. Alex then went to Markeaton primary school that was well-resourced for his needs.

The Education Authority didn't want me to go straight up to Markeaton primary school the same as Alex as my vision wasn't as bad as his, but

Mum told them, "Well if you think I am going through the same with Keri as I went through with Alex you have got another thing coming."

Markeaton primary school is in Derby so Alex and I used to go in a taxi, provided by the Education Authority, which we shared with other children and an escort. Mum found it really hard the first year Alex was at Markeaton primary school not being able to take him to school like before. Any friends that Alex and I had from infant's school thought Alex and I had just gone to a different junior school from them rather than a special school. It wasn't until Mum saw their parents when she was out and they enquired after Alex and I that they found out where we had gone. Our previous friends used to come round to our house in the evenings and enquire if we would go and play on the road with them, when we explained that we couldn't because of our sight they weren't bothered and stopped coming round!

Every year during one particular weekend in May, we used to go to Lea Green with the VI (visually impaired) unit for the weekend. Mum and Dad used to take Alex and I to Markeaton primary school on Friday where we would all meet up ready to go to Lea Green. On the Friday when we got there we just used to acquaint ourselves with the place we were staying. On the Saturday we used to go for a walk and take camping equipment with us and have a BBQ for dinner. After dinner we used to go on the rope course there which was good fun. On the Sunday we used to go for a stream walk in our wellingtons which was good fun even though we used to get a little wet.

Every academic year we used to go out with the Kids Day Out charity with a friend of our choice with the other visually impaired children. We chose to go to the American Adventure for the day.

Every Friday afternoon all the visually impaired children used to play on the soft play area which I really enjoyed.

All the VI children used to be supported in some lessons such as P.E. and science, to some degree depending on their disability, where there was an element of risk.

When my vision started to deteriorate to the point where I couldn't see my pencil I was given a pencil with a thicker lead and I sat near the blackboard so I could see it easily. At junior school I didn't really like the Maths books we used to work from called Peak (1, 2, 3 etc) part (1 or 2). In my last year I started having to use the CCTV to see the book. I never liked the Reading Routes that we did for English that worked on comprehension, which I think was due to me having to concentrate so hard on seeing the information that I couldn't take it in, so I used to struggle to answer the questions. In the library they had quite a few large print books but I was unable to read the print by the end of junior school as I couldn't read them without using the CCTV to help. I spent a lot of time looking through the library for books with bigger print in sometimes having to get children's books since the print was bigger in these.

In my second year I struggled with my blood sugars going low and due to this I used to get double vision which made writing in certain boxes difficult. I also started to struggle with my hearing and this was when I started wearing hearing aids.

Every week we used to have spellings to learn for the Friday when we had a spelling test. One week the spellings included both witch and which and in the spelling test the teacher just said the word with no clues i.e. witch with a broom and the question which, so I didn't know which went where. When I got my spellings marked I got 8 out of 10 as I had put the two words in the wrong place—this really annoyed me. I used to struggle to spell words like used as I thought it ought to be spelt 'yoused'. On Tuesday afternoons we used to be taught by another teacher and we learned how to make things like kaleidoscopes (I hate that spelling!) On a Thursday morning after break, we used to have P.E. with Mrs Robinson who was a teacher that worked at the school on Thursdays and Fridays. Mrs Robinson was a strict but fair teacher. Once in P.E. she shouted at the group of children and because it made me jump it upset me, but after this we got on really well.

In Maths I used to struggle to understand why the number 12 was even as it starts with a 1.

I remember doing a test in year 5 where we had to put fractions in order of biggest to smallest which I got totally wrong thinking 1 was smaller than 1/3 as I didn't understand fractions then. One of my aunts taught me how fractions worked by getting some sweets and getting me to work out how many sweets made half a portion etc.

Due to the condition Alex and I have we both have lowered immunity. In my fourth year I went down with a virus where I was tired a lot and had about a month off school. When I went back to school I was still suffering with being tired, but not as much—as time went by I got better. On Thursday mornings before break, Mrs Robinson used to teach us Maths.

Even then Alex and I had quite a few hospital appointments to attend. Mum used to fetch Alex and I from school to attend hospital appointments which we had to catch the bus to as Mum can't drive (except for round the bend or up the wall!) If the appointment was in the morning Mum used to take us to school after the appointment.

Also in year 4 we learned about Egypt and mummies and we used to have to practise being a mummy in drama which I didn't like—I still don't like drama now! I didn't like learning music apart from singing! With school we used to go swimming at the local swimming baths—about the only thing I didn't like about that were the caps we wore to keep our hair dry. I used to do some physio at break times once a week, with some other children to help our balance.

In P.E. we sometimes played rounders which I wasn't very good at as I used to get mixed up between who were standing as markers of the circle to run round and who were fielding! In breaks we sometimes played British bulldog or Stuck in the mud where we used to have to go down on one knee if we were caught and could be set free by somebody in our team touching us.

I met my best friend Jenny in my first year in junior school and I am still best friends with her now. When we went out to play we used to go on disco hoppers and bounce around the house outside or on the field together which I really enjoyed.   Now we see each other once a month where either she comes to my house or I go to hers.   When we spend the day together we play scrabble a lot where Jenny sometimes beats me—one of the few people who can beat me at scrabble.   Jenny and I always go out for a meal every time we spend the day together.   Sometimes Jenny and I go to Alton Towers together where she enjoys going on all the rides I like. Sometimes if Jenny can't come with me to Alton Towers I go with a carer from an agency that I get care from.

Jenny and I went through junior school in the same class as each other up until our final year, where one teacher in her wisdom decided to separate us.   My teacher kept telling Mum at parents' evenings that I hadn't settled very well and Mum kept telling her it was because she had split me and Jenny up.   The teacher used to say, "Well they will be separated next year as they are going to different senior schools," and Mum's response was, "Yes, but you could have left them together for the last year!" Mum and this teacher had an unspoken dislike for each other and agreed to disagree about this.

Towards the end of junior school I stopped being able to see my pencil so I used a fine liner to write with and had to get work sheets enlarged or read things under the CCTV.   Throughout junior school Alex and I started to learn Braille at a slow rate because we weren't sure how fast our vision would deteriorate.   All through junior school we both learned to touch type so we could use a computer when we couldn't see.   One of the programs we used for touch typing used to say a letter and we had to press that letter, this was OK if you could hear which letter it was asking you to press, but I couldn't very well so I used to get frustrated with it.

In May of year 6 my grandma died in hospital which I knew about even without anybody telling me as I have ESP (extrasensory perception) the same as Mum.   I remember getting home and Dad informed me that Mum was on the way back home but not to expect good news.   That night I remember watching 'Lord of the Dance' and being really upset.

Chapter 9

Social Groups

When I was 6, I started going to Rainbows with Natalie and some girls from school, where we used to play games. One game we played was Hide and Seek and we used to hide in a dark side room, but I used to worry about not being found and sit waiting even when the others were doing something else, so I used to come out from hiding just in case and found out we were still playing. After a time I stopped going because I found it too scary.

I then started going to Sunday school at my local church just so I was meeting children the same age as me. I used to like Sunday school and the things we used to do. A volunteer from our local church who ran the Sunday school, used to pick me up for Sunday school and then bring me back home.

When Alex and I started secondary school we used to go to swimming club at our local swimming pool. I used to like swimming but I always struggled to get my legs right when I was doing breast stroke. When the instructor was talking to the group Alex always made sure I was near the front so I could hear, since I couldn't wear my hearing aids when swimming. I really enjoyed swimming club until they decided that to save money they would merge the swimming club groups from different nights into one night. This meant that instead of there being about 6 in a lane there were 10. I used to get that fed up of banging into other people all the time that I couldn't concentrate on swimming. I eventually got out the pool one evening because I was upset and I never went again after this.

When I was 8 years old I started Brownies where I used to have a lady supporting me so I could join in with the other children and do what they were doing. After a year I transferred from Brownies to Guides.

When I was 9 years old I enrolled as a member of my local guide group. Guides used to be held on a Monday evening between 7.30pm and 9.00pm after Brownies. As my chronic fatigue started to get worse, I still used to go to Guides but Mum used to pick me up at 8.30pm so I could be in bed for 9.00pm, which even then used to be a late night for me. With Guides I used to work towards badges the same as the other members and take part in the same activities. The Guides leader called Mandy used to work at a School with blind people so she knew how to help me. She got me a large print handbook and used to put me in patrols where there was an older guide who could help me. Mum used to walk me round to my friend Kirsty's house and then we used to walk to the church where Guides was run from to give me some independence.

A few times I went camping with Guides at the weekend to Drum Hill, which is not far from Ilkeston. At Drum Hill I used to stop in the same tent as the Guide Leader so she could help me during the night to go across to the local toilets. On Saturday we were taken to a wood where we used to have to find a flower for each of the colours of the rainbow. It was then that one of the older guides taught me the proper colours of the rainbow and the rhyme of how to remember them which went as follows:
Richard of York gave battle in vain
Red, orange, yellow, green, blue, indigo and violet.

In the afternoon we used to go abseiling down a tower that we had to first climb up by a really steep ladder. The first time I went abseiling the instructor came down with me to give me confidence. I haven't been abseiling for a long time but I used to really enjoy it.

Also with Guides I went to the Czech Republic twice. Both times we went we did pretty much the same things, but the first time the Guide Leader looked after me. The second time, because my condition was worse, I had another carer with me. In the Czech Republic we stayed in a cottage and the first time I went I fell down a flight of marble steps, but landed on my bottom sitting up—I just bruised my back. We went to Prague twice, to the crystal factory and to see a show where we had dinner one evening. The second time I went I twisted my ankle getting off the coach the same evening we saw the show, and then at dinner I started feeling not very well, nearly the whole Guide group went down with a sickness bug. We all had to go to the doctors and have an injection to stop us being sick any more. During the night they had to have the ambulance out to me twice because of me being very unwell and having diabetes, which meant that they had to give them the last of the Guides 'just in case' money.   Luckily Mum didn't know anything about this until I got home.

Chapter 10
Secondary School

Before Alex and I started senior school we both had mobility lessons to familiarise us with the layout of the school so that when we started we knew where everything was.

Alex and I went to Saint Benedict's School in Derby which is not far from Markeaton primary school. We used to get a taxi to school each day which we shared with other children but by this age we didn't need an escort to take us.

At secondary school Alex and I started learning Braille at a quicker rate as our vision was getting worse. At this point I needed work to be enlarged from n12 to n24 so I could read it, but even then I couldn't read for a long time as it used to make my eyes tired. Sometimes in English they used to set us some homework to read so much of a certain book. I used to start reading it but Mum had to read the rest to me. I really started to like Maths in year 7 and I really liked the teacher too.

In year 7 I sometimes used to go to school without my hearing aids in by mistake as my hearing wasn't too bad at that time but I noticed a little difference in volume, luckily Mum and Dad used to bring them to me. Near the end of year 7 I started struggling with my energy levels—falling to sleep in some lessons when I should have been listening to the teacher. Once in music we were watching a video but because I was so tired I fell asleep by accident and when I woke up near the end my friends asked me if I had a nice sleep. This made me really embarrassed as I was hoping nobody had noticed!

In February of 1998 when I was in year 7 we started having an extension at home to make the front room and our bedrooms bigger. Whilst this was happening Alex and I both went down with the flu which was a nightmare. We used to have to rest in the front room as our bedrooms were out of bounds as well as the bathroom. We had to go across to our neighbour (Kath) to use her toilet as we couldn't get to ours. Once when

Mum took one of us across to the toilet Mum said, "It is lovely and warm in here," and Kath enquired if we had any heating and Mum explained we couldn't use it because of the extension so she told Mum to fetch the other child. When we were both across at Kath's house Alex and I promptly fell asleep whilst Mum was talking to Kath. When Kath used to go out she left Mum her key so we could still use her toilet. Once when Mum took us to the doctors the doctor enquired if we were getting plenty of rest and Mum told her that we couldn't go to bed as she and Dad had to take our beds apart each day and then put them back together at night. On the day when the middle wall was knocked through it was awful as brick dust went everywhere. Mum had to get our aunt to take us to her house whilst she and Dad tidied the house from top to bottom.

From then on the doctor told us to take 500 mg vitamin C a day. We used to take Haliborange each day so Mum said jokingly, "That's it, keep shovelling them in," and the doctor said, "No, just one tablet!" We also had our flu jab each year. I have sometimes had a reaction to the flu jab but I haven't had flu again.

In year 7 I did CDT (creative design technology) where I made a letter rack with a flower on it but because I wasn't very organised then, I kept losing bits, so I had to repeat things. I was late finishing the letter rack so I didn't get time to do the write up whilst at school so I had to do it for homework. On this night I did an hour's work before going to Guides. When I got back from Guides I went straight to bed as it was 9 o'clock which was late for me. The next day at school my ECO (education care officer) wanted to know why the write up wasn't completed so I explained that I went to Guides and then I went to bed. She wanted to know why I didn't complete it after Guides!

At the end of year 7 I went to France with other children from my year and another visually impaired girl called Leanne. Two ECOs (education care officers) went with us to France. Dad had to take me early one morning to school to catch the bus to France and because of my medication I had two bags with me. Dad told my ECO that my bags needed to be with me at all times as it had medication in it which I needed during the day and the ECO said they would put it in the boot and stop the bus when I needed

58

it. On the way to France Leanne and I sat together on the coach whilst our ECOs were further down the bus. On the way I listened to my personal stereo and sang along to the songs until Leanne told me that other people didn't appreciate it as they were trying to listen to a tape that was being played on the coach—I hadn't thought of that. When we stopped at the services Leanne and I got our dinner with help and then we were sitting at a table waiting for the ECOs to join us. After waiting a while we decided to eat our meal as the ECOs hadn't joined us. I remember going across to France on the ferry but I can't remember much else. When we got to our hotel in France it was quite late so we had something to eat and then went to bed. Each morning and evening when I needed to do my blood sugars and injection I went apart from everybody else with my ECO to do them. The next day we went to Disneyland where we spent most of the morning following our ECO round looking in shops as we thought our ECO would accompany us to the rides we wanted to go on. At one point I told her that I needed the toilet but instead of finding one quickly for me the ECO carried on looking at things so I ended up wetting myself. In the afternoon Leanne and I went off with another girl in our year and got the sky ride to another part of Disneyland but there was a queue so we didn't get chance to go on any rides. By the time we got back to the meeting point to catch the bus back our ECO was waiting for us as we were late. That evening we went back to Disneyland to see the firework display and had a walk back. Whilst we were out it absolutely threw it down with rain and we all got really wet. When we got on the coach they had the blowers on to dry us but it felt cold. By the time we got back to the hotel it was 11 o'clock but they wanted us to write a log—needless to say I said no. The following day we went to the Eiffel Tower to have a look and then we set off back home. On the way back on the coach I said I needed my medication which was in the boot. They moaned about stopping the coach as they were worried about us missing the Eurostar back to England but they stopped and got it for me. Also on the way back I moaned once that it was too noisy on the bus and I was trying to sleep but they just told me to take my hearing aids out which didn't help much at that time because I could still hear quite well without them. I eventually got back to school with everybody else and Dad came to fetch me—I had enjoyed it but it was very tiring.

On the Tuesday Mrs Gorman (head of the VI unit) wanted to see Leanne and I after lunch—I knew I was in trouble but I didn't know what for. When Leanne and I went after lunch Mrs Gorman had a right moan at us saying we had spoiled it for the ECOs and moaned at us for a lot of things. When I got back home I was still in tears and told Mum what had happened. Mum asked Mrs Gorman for a list of the things she had moaned at us about so she could go through them with me. Mrs Gorman sent the letter home to Mum on the last day of term. On the list were things like; not being able to find toilets in Disneyland, that I needed too much looking after, about me complaining about noise level, couldn't follow clear instructions given on a noisy bus, needed the bus stopping for my medication and nearly fell down steps.

Mum was seething when she read this list and wrote a letter explaining that; Dad had told them that I needed my medication with me at all times, school only saw the finished article when I went but not all the looking after I needed, couldn't see well enough to find toilets on my own, needed long cane training so I wouldn't fall down steps, needed my hearing testing by hearing specialist at school. Mum sent this to the headmaster who just said it was a learning curve for staff and students!

When Mum next saw Mrs Gorman and gave her the letter Mum said to Mrs Gorman that instead of moaning about things do something about them. Mrs Gorman told Mum that she worried too much. After this Mrs Gorman gave Mum her home phone number so Mum could ring her if there were any problems and Mum and Mrs Gorman had regular meetings to discuss any problems. Mum told Alex and I if there were any problems at school to tell her and she would write them down to discuss at the next meeting where she took her notepad. After the France trip Mum and Mrs Gorman didn't get on very well for a few years.

In year 8 I started having to drop some subjects so I had time during the day to either have a rest or do my homework at school so I could rest when I got home, as I was too tired to work all day and then do homework when I got home. The first few subjects I dropped were CDT, drama, music and textiles. In year 8 I started to do long cane training in mobility so I could use a long cane instead of just carrying a symbol cane around with me because by then I couldn't see kerbs and steps. I used to do P.E. and mobility training twice a week, but I had to cut down to once a week because they were making me too tired. Mum arranged this with Mrs Gorman but for some reason the other members of staff didn't know about it. One day I went into school and my ECO (education care officer) wanted to know why I hadn't brought my P.E. kit with me. When I tried explaining that I didn't do P.E. any more she got angry with me and upset me. At home I told Mum about this so she wrote me a note in my school homework book for next week. The following week my ECO got annoyed again so I thrust my homework book in her face and showed her Mum's note which she took and showed another ECO. The other ECO came in and said that they didn't know anything about this. When I told Mum she rang Mrs Gorman the next day and told her who sorted it out.

At the end of year 8 the Visually Impaired Unit arranged a holiday away from the Wednesday to the Friday where we went to a cottage in Buxton. Whilst we were there we were put into pairs with the other children to carry out the cooking, pot washing and setting the table and this was done on a rota. On the Wednesday evening Alex and I went for a walk nearby and walked through a wood and up to a castle. When we got back and told them all where we had been they decided to go there the next evening for a walk all together. On the Thursday we went into Matlock to have a walk by the canal and we went in the park. On the Friday we just packed everything and went back to school. When we got back to school the headmaster saw us unpacking the minibus and asked if we had been away and what we had done.

Also in year 8 a hearing advisory teacher used to come to test my hearing and she gave me a radio aid where I wore a receiver and the teacher wore the transmitter, which meant that the teacher's voice went straight into my hearing aid so I could hear better. Near the end of year 8 I was diagnosed Multi-Sensory Impaired and the MSI teacher used to come to see me at school once a week to see how I was doing.

By the middle of year 9 I couldn't see print so I had to transfer over to Braille which luckily I had already learned. I really struggled in year 9 coming up to my SATs because I had to concentrate that hard on what the

Braille said that I couldn't take in what I was being taught. In my Maths SATs I did really well especially in the mental arithmetic test where I got the answer really quick and didn't need all my allotted time.

In my options I just picked the core curriculum so I could concentrate on the subjects and have free sessions during the day to do my homework. By this time I had decided that I wanted to go to university but I wasn't sure what to study yet. During year 10 I started helping to teach Braille to other people who were learning Braille as I wanted to help people. In year 10 I did the junior maths challenge with people in my Maths group and I got a bronze certificate which I was really pleased about. At the end of year 10 I went on work experience to the NRSB (Nottingham Royal Society for the Blind) where I did a mixture of activities like teaching Braille, proof reading Braille and I spent one morning in the nursery—never again! At that time my granddad used to go there once a week to the centre for a social group and one day I joined him for lunch which I enjoyed.

At the end of that year when I did my exams I got A* in Maths. In the summer of 2001 I went to the Czech Republic with Guides and fractured my ankle on the last day. When I got home I went to the doctors who sent me for an X-ray and I had to have my foot in pot for quite a while. Due to my balance I couldn't use crutches so I used a Zimmer frame which was fun! At school they wouldn't let me use the Zimmer frame and because I wouldn't use a wheelchair I walked on it which made the pot crack, so I had to have a new one done.

All the way through school my favourite subject was Maths as it had been ever since infant school. I never liked English especially not Shakespeare but I had never enjoyed studying English right from being at junior school. Once I started learning just biology in years 10 and 11 I really enjoyed it. Learning French wasn't one of my favourite subjects but I preferred it to the depth we studied English. I never really enjoyed R.E. up until I got into year 10 when we studied Mark's Gospel which I really enjoyed. At the end of year 11 I did my G.C.S.E.s where I got A in Maths, B in Biology, C in French, C in R.E., C in English Language and D in English Literature. I was never very good at remembering to write what homework I had got in my homework log book as I remembered it so well when I thought of what lessons I had had that day.

I particularly remember my Sixth Form Induction Day because this was the day my granddad died. I remember having a dream (as I thought) about Dad not coming home and I remember thinking "Don't be silly he is in bed with Mum" but I was seeing it through Mum's eyes as granddad was on holiday when he died—so yes his body came back but he never came back as I remember him. Mum had to take me to school on the bus because the LEA wouldn't fund me to go in a taxi. When Mum and I were on the bus Mum got a phone call on her mobile from her brother telling her the bad news and when she said, "Oh my god" I knew what he had told Mum. After Mum had dropped me off at school and we had had a talk with Mrs Gorman, Mum went back into Derby for a walk round. I didn't stay all day at the Induction Day but just until after dinner when Mum came and fetched me. At the Induction Day I met up with the head of the Maths Department and talked to her about me studying A level Maths and I saw the I.T. teacher about the AVCE (Advanced Vocational Certificate in Education) I.T. that I wanted to study. I then went on to study A level Maths in Sixth Form at school and AVCE I.T. In Maths I still had the same Maths teacher and I did really well in the first few books that we studied. I preferred the Pure Maths to Statistics even though I did well in both areas. In I.T. I studied different types of communication produced using I.T., Excel and I.T. used in companies. In Sixth Form everybody was required to do a Student Assistance Placement so in my first and second year I helped teach Braille and in my third year I helped support a student in Maths. To help get more information about different universities I got a UCAS card where universities would send me information about their courses.

Throughout Sixth Form I visited several universities as well as going to an office in Derby to talk to somebody about being an accountant. After I had spoken to several people I decided not to study accountancy at university, otherwise I could only go into accountancy, but to study Maths so I would have more options. People also advised me against being an accountant as I would be stuck in an office not seeing many people. After visiting 3 universities I eventually chose Sheffield as my first choice and Loughborough as my second choice.

In April I went to Sheffield, Hallam University to have my assessment of needs which would decide how much care I needed and how much disabled students allowance (DSA) I would get.   I ended up getting the full amount of DSA but even this wasn't enough, so the university ended up having to pay towards my care.   The plan was for the course material to start being put into Braille since I had already decided I wanted to go there.   When my Sixth Form exam results came out I didn't quite meet the grades that the university wanted, so I might have had to go through some of the clearing process—I am not sure now.

Chapter 11

University

When I eventually started university I hadn't quite received all of the equipment I was supposed to receive and this took some time to come. Right from starting university I didn't receive any course material in Braille but I didn't make a fuss about it straight away as I thought it was just teething problems. In the module Mathematical Modelling I decided to become a Student Representative. As part of being a Student Rep, I had to go to the student union where I learned about what services they offered.

I was having to bring print worksheets home for Mum to read out to me so I could try to do some homework. This was difficult because Mum hadn't done Maths for 35 years so she had to describe the symbols to me, then read a sheet to me and then I had to Braille it which took an hour per page! My notes in classes were being taken by note takers (ones without any Maths background), and were initially being sent to the Braille Transcription Centre. The university had employed somebody to Braille my notes for me but unknown to me at the time this wasn't happening. After several weeks of this I tried calling a meeting with everybody I thought needed to attend the meeting—I never realised how hard it was trying to get everybody in the same place at once! I reduced my modules hoping that this would give the Braille chance to catch up. I then decided to go to the Student Union and talk to somebody about the problems I was having and I saw an educational guide who helped me decide what my choices were. By December I was really upset and stressed about how things were turning out and I was due to have some exams in January so I arranged another meeting. Mum came to this meeting with me and told them what she thought of it and I decided to temporarily withdraw from university.

When I had withdrawn I rang the Disability Discrimination Act (DDA) adviser and they put me in touch with the Disability Reconciliation Service (DRS) who liaised between me and the university. In the meantime the lady in the Student Union at university helped me get some compensation from the university because of all my struggles.

At that time Alex was at the RNIB (Royal National Institute for the Blind) Loughborough College who had an open day in February. At the open day a teacher told Mum about the adult I.T. course they were running. As I wasn't at university then I decided to go to the job centre to see if I could get funding so I could attend this course, staying residential during the week and going home at weekends. Whilst I was waiting for the funding to come through a meeting was arranged at a neutral location for me to attend with Mum with some people from the university's Disabled Support Team and the lady from the DRS.

At the meeting the people from the university first thanked us for not putting them in the paper and Mum said that that would be her next move if they didn't sort things out. Then they explained that the person who they had employed to do the Brailling had been on long-term sick but they had been expecting them in at some point; unfortunately they had died. They were employing two people who had done Maths themselves to take notes for me and support me in classes and tutorials. The reason why they hadn't already started Brailling the course notes from the previous year ready for me was because every 5 years the course has to be revised and unfortunately for me that was the year.

When I got the funding to start my course, I borrowed quite a lot of stuff off Alex, since he was at college as well. Alex asked me at one point what I was taking of my own and I said, "I am taking my best friend," (meaning Cadbury my teddy!) and Alex said, "Well I am not going," I said, "That's because you're not my best friend," and Alex went, "Huh." The day I started residential college I got really upset when I went to give Mum a kiss and cuddle because rather than saying, "See you tonight," I had to say, "See you on Friday." I cried all the way to college and didn't calm down until people from the college started talking to me. That evening when I was across at the residential place, rather than staying in my room on my own I went into the lounge part and started talking to a boy there. From that night on I started playing games with 2 other boys in the evening which I really enjoyed. When I told Mum about the boys

I was playing games with, Mum said, "I will have to keep an eye on you with all these boys around!" At the college I learned how to use Excel, Database Manager, write coding to create Websites and some other things which came in useful at university.

When I started back at university the following September 2 people, Eric and Jo, had been trained up in how to prepare and Braille my course material and notes for me. Eric and Jo had both studied Maths at a high level so they knew all the symbols and could take down notes and equations for me. In lectures I either had Jo or Eric taking my notes for me and they would support me in tutorials and give me extra learning support sessions as well as preparing my notes for me. I also had a personal assistant with me all the time guiding me from place to place during the day. When I got to university each day in a taxi, (no I didn't have to pay for the taxi myself. The LEA paid for most of it. I just had to contribute £9.50 is what it would cost somebody to travel to university on public transport), the personal assistant would meet me 15 minutes before my first lecture/support session to give us time to get there. I had weekly meetings with the head of the Maths Department, called Neil, who would sort out any problems straight away rather than me having to arrange a meeting. I studied 90 credits a year instead of 120 credits so it wouldn't make me too tired. As a result of this it took me 4 years to complete the course instead of 3 years. I could have taken a year's placement as part of the course but I just wanted to get the course finished. I received double the time to do my exams, as everybody else, which sometimes meant it would go over the 3 hours that I could cope with in a day, due to getting tired. To get over this problem there were a few options that the university gave me; doing the exam over 2 days, doing half assignment and half exam or the tutor taking out questions so it only took 3 hours for me to do, which was OK as long as I liked the questions the tutor gave me! I knew that if the tutor chose the questions there might be some I was good at, so I would get top marks, or they could all be ones I didn't like, so I wouldn't do very well. I used to enjoy doing exams. I liked the idea of getting the exam done rather than spending a long time on coursework. In one assignment that I did in year 3 I got 100 percent and Alex commented that he was surprised I could fit through the door because of my big head!

In the last year of the course I was starting to get really tired and by March I had to have 3 weeks off for Easter instead of 2 as my health wasn't very good—it took me 2 days to get over going to university for a day, so I was playing catch up all the time!

At the end of the first year of university I got a phone call from the Loughborough RNIB College saying that the Braille teacher that had worked there had died, so they asked me to work there until I went back to university, one day a week which I got paid for. At the end of year 2 I did a week's work experience at the Department of Work and Pensions, working with the statisticians where I worked a little on analysing data and a bit on using the SAS (statistical analysis software). I was OK with recognising which part of the SAS code I needed for what I was doing, but I couldn't remember the code well enough to write my own code down. To get to the DWP which was based in Sheffield I had care from an agency and they took me to Derby train station and we got a train to Sheffield where we got a taxi to the DWP.

At university my favourite modules were those using equations and solving them. Quite a few modules involved modelling equations on the computer that I wasn't very keen on. In my final year I had to choose a project to study. Most of the projects were based on modelling but there were two that didn't called Relativity or Quantum Theory. I decided to study the project on Quantum Theory where I had an equation to solve and multiplying the equation by other equations. I found out later that the course I had chosen to do was concentrated on Applied Maths where you use a lot of modelling, which I didn't realise. Perhaps if I had done more research before I applied to study that course I would have found out, but I just wanted to find a course to do at a university where they would accept me on the grades I could get! At Sixth Form and university I chose to study Maths and Statistics rather than Maths and Engineering as I thought the latter would involve a lot of nuts, screws and bolts.

Chapter 12
Social Care

When Alex and I were young we didn't need too much looking after and only needed our blood sugars checking before Mum and Dad went to bed and then in the morning. We didn't need looking after too much during the day as we were at school full time so Mum and Dad only needed to do things with us at weekends and evenings. In the evenings I used to go across the road and play with Matthew and Natalie quite a bit and go to Brownies or Guides. Sometimes Alex and I used to listen to videos or telly with Mum and Dad or on our own. When Alex and I started having low blood sugars at night, or hypos, Mum realised that we needed our blood sugars checking more regularly. So Mum started testing our blood sugars more during the night.

After Alex and I were diagnosed with this condition we used to have a lady from the Diabetic clinic come to our house and counsel us as well as Mum. When Alex was about 12 she started to find counselling us both too difficult so Alex used to go and see someone else. Unfortunately a lady called Kath went off work with back pains when I was 14 years old. When I was 13 I was diagnosed multi-sensory impaired and a lady called Mandy used to come to see me once a week at school to help me. Unfortunately Mandy stopped coming to see me around the same time as Kath stopped too. I now keep in touch with Kath as a friend and we go out about once a month for a meal and a chat. Luckily Mum managed to find somewhere else that provided counselling, where a taxi would pick me up from school or home and take me to the appointment and then take me wherever I needed to go. I enjoyed going to see Malcolm which was once a week as it gave me chance to discuss my problems. Unfortunately Malcolm went off with depression when I was 20 years old. Luckily Alex was already seeing Dr Swanwick at Ilkeston hospital and she agreed to counsel me. In 2015 Dr Swanwick stopped providing counselling at the hospital and Alex and I were left without a counsellor to see. Since then I have been to see somebody from the Mental Health Service for 2 lots of 6 weeks and I know it is there when I need it.

When I was about 10 Mum and Dad went to the York Cycle Rally which is held over a weekend in June. Mum and Dad decided to go there so they could have a break from looking after us all the time, so Alex and I slept over at my grandparents' house. Mum found out later that grandma ended up sleeping in the landing between our bedrooms so she could keep an eye on us both, so Mum looked into what other care was available. The following year we started having a nurse from the City Hospital coming to stay with us over the weekend whilst Mum and Dad went away, which worked really well. Whilst the nurse was with us we used to go on days out. The nurse used to look after our diabetes and do our meals for us which was good as it allowed Mum and Dad to have a weekend's break without having to worry about us. We didn't just have her once but for a couple of years or so which allowed us to get to know each other really well. One time when she came to look after Alex and I over the weekend Alex wasn't very well and his blood sugars were high so he needed looking after even more than usual but Mum and Dad still got their well-deserved break as they knew we were being looked after. After a few years she left but another nurse came to stay with us whilst Mum and Dad were away, of whom we got on well. For some reason the nurses stopped coming to us and we got a letter from the Group saying they had stopped coming as we had cancelled them which was wrong.

Luckily our social worker at this time knew about a charity called Barnardo's, who did a link scheme where I could go to stay with a family for the weekend and they would get paid to look after me whilst Mum and Dad had a break, and the same applied to Alex so we would have a break from each other too. I had a choice of two families to go to, one of whom lived in Belper and the other lived in Alfreton. When I went to stay with the family in Belper we used to go out for walks in the countryside which I used to enjoy. When I went to the family in Alfreton we used to play a lot of board games and do a lot of cooking which I really enjoyed too.

Unfortunately this all stopped when we went into adult services and they gave us no alternatives. Also at this time Alex had finished secondary school so Mum had to look after him during the day as well as checking our blood sugars 3 times a night. As you can imagine this made Mum really tired all the time but what else could she do! Luckily my Aunty

Marian only lived in the next village from us so we used to go to her house on Sundays whilst Mum and Dad went on the tandem. At Aunty Marian's house we used to have dinner and go out with her and my Uncle Geoff to take their dog for a walk. Sometimes we didn't both take their dog for a walk, as I stayed with Aunty Marian and had a really good talk about everything whilst Alex wasn't there.

Once Alex and I went into adult services we stopped getting any night time or day time care so Mum and Dad had to do it all. After about a year Dad heard an advert on the radio about this agency called 24/7. Mum arranged for somebody from there to come and see us but they failed to come twice in a row, not a good sign! After telling our social worker about this he suggested that we contacted an agency called Mediline which we did. The Nursing Director came out to see us from Mediline and did an assessment of our needs and we have been having care from them ever since; we have had a nurse 5 nights a week and Mum does the other two nights. As Alex and I need our blood sugars checking every 2 hours at night the nurse does a waking night. Our Diabetes consultant has been involved in ensuring that we still get the funding for the nurses even today.

Whilst I was still at university I only received care once a week or when Mum and Dad went on the tandem. I still carried on going to Aunty Marian's house when Mum and Dad went out at weekends instead of having care up until Aunty Marian moved down to Norfolk—it was a bit too far to go then! Since leaving university I have had care Monday to Friday for 4 or so hours a day just to get me out and give Mum some space. I don't have care at weekends as I like spending time with Mum and Dad. For the last few years I have had to pay so much towards my care costs each week, but not too much thankfully.

Up until I was 10 years old we had a car that was our own that Dad had bought. Unfortunately in 1997 our car failed its MOT and it would cost more money to mend it than to get a new car. As I was already receiving a high rate of the mobility component of DLA (Disability Living Allowance), Mum rang them up to see if it was possible for us to get a second-hand car. When Mum rang up they asked if there was any chance of my vision getting better and Mum replied, "Yes, if there is a bolt from the blue!" so they sent Mum a form to fill out. When we went to get the car we ended up with a new car that we have to change every 3 years. On the form that the man from Motability fills out every 3 years, it asks if the owner (me) will be driving the car and he always says, "Oh dear, I think I better put no there!" We don't have to worry about taxing or insuring the car as all the services and MOTs are included in the allowance. When the car needs servicing they come and collect the car and bring it back when they have finished.

Now I have a car which I use when I have care and this gives me chance to go wherever I want (within reason!) I go all over the place in it now, going to see friends like Shirley and an old school teacher and I get up to lots of mischief!

Chapter 13

After University

When I finished university in September 2010 I said, "Right, I am not doing any more studying!" After I had made this decision I got rid of all my notes I didn't need and my big Braille folders.

I then decided I wanted to teach Braille to people so I applied at a few places like my own primary school and secondary school but other LSA's were doing that. This annoyed me as they could do everything else that I couldn't do so why couldn't they let me do what I could do—like teaching Braille! After talking to people I eventually approached the Nottingham City Council to see if I could become a volunteer for teaching people Braille. After going to talk to the person in charge at the Nottingham City Council I became a volunteer.

My decision not to study lasted until February the next year when I decided I was bored and I wanted to study something—not at university but at college. After thinking this through I thought of studying the PTLLS (Preparing to Teach in the Lifelong Learning Sector) course at Loughborough College. The idea to study at Loughborough College was based on the idea that the RNIB (Royal National Institute for the Blind) Loughborough College was next door and they could prepare my notes and course material in Braille and provide me with a note taker. I then applied to the Gardeners Trust for funding and the college to get on the course. I started my course in June 2011 with my note taker and carer along with other sighted students. Throughout my course I had to have some teaching hours so I could prepare a scheme of work, lesson plans and lesson notes. Not long before I started this course the Nottingham City Council asked me to meet a lady called Shirley who wanted to learn Braille, to see if we would get on.

Ever since Shirley and I first met we got on like a house on fire—it was just one of those meetings where you know as soon as you meet.

Having Shirley to teach Braille to gave me the hours work experience I needed to prepare the documents for my course. Throughout this course we had to write 6 assignments and then at the end of the course we each had to do a 20 minute lesson on the topic of our choice. Unfortunately the morning I should have done my tutorial I wasn't very well so I had to do my tutorial last. I had chosen to do my tutorial on simultaneous equations which I really liked. I did print and Braille on card and took blue tack to stick them on the blackboard and I kept asking my classmates questions. Unfortunately this was a very difficult topic for most people so only a couple of people answered the questions and I didn't think to ask other people—I was just glad people were answering my questions. In this course you could either do level 3 or 4 and then depending on how good the work is depends on whether you need to do the CTLLS (Certificate in Teaching in the Lifelong Learning Sector) or go straight onto doing the DTLLS (Diploma in Teaching in the Lifelong Learning Sector). I got level 3 which I wasn't too worried about as I had planned to do the CTLLS anyway. I then applied to the Ilkeston Rotary Club for funding to study the CTLLS where I had to go and give a talk.

Throughout the CTLLS course we also had to teach so I carried on teaching to Shirley. At the end of each lesson we received an assignment to complete where we had to answer three questions. In the last question we had to apply it to our own teaching and then we had to present this to the rest of the group. I really enjoyed the assignments and I really felt like I didn't do too badly with the presentation. I really felt a part of the group when students used to ask me questions instead of waiting for the teacher because they knew I remembered things really well. In the group there was one student who was from the PTLLS group I went to which made it nice to have a familiar face (well you know what I mean). During some of the classes we had to do some group work which I used to help with using my note taker and then we had to present what we had done. During the presentation I introduced the topic and then explained that I couldn't take part in the rest as it wasn't in Braille. When it came to finishing the course we were told that the rules had changed that year so that we could graduate from doing the CTLLS, so I then graduated again.

Before last October Mum had a wall full of my graduation photos but now that wall has got my brother's photos on—I will say why later.

After trying several gyms that were public I eventually started at the local David Lloyd gym which is a private gym as I liked the layout and thought these activities that I could do with my carers help so I used to go there once a week. Together with going to the gym, teaching Shirley Braille and going to "'ave a go" I had a busy structured week which I really enjoyed.

Unfortunately in September 2014 "'ave a go" closed which I found really annoying as I really enjoyed going there. Luckily about the same time the doctors surgery started doing a "craft and chatter" group which Alex and I used to go to together. All the facilities were really good. I used to go once a week to the gym with my carer together with Shirley and her carer. I really enjoyed going to the gym as it gave me something to do that I enjoyed and my carer could join in as well—the only trouble was it was quite expensive. In March 2014 I started going to the "'ave a go" place in Ilkeston where they had lots of art that you could do like making greeting cards, painting things and making clay imprints. I used to enjoy making clay imprints where I could push a cutter into the clay and then once it was dry I could paint it. I have always enjoyed making greeting cards but the problem was having somebody to do it with.

Chapter 14

Medical Problems Now

In 2007 I had my tonsils out and the bore holes at the top of my nose made wider as I had suffered from sinusitis for many years, having to have a lot of time off school. At first I didn't like the sounds of just having my bore holes made wider under a general anaesthetic so when I realised I needed to have my tonsils out it was a case of killing two birds with one stone. When I came home after having the operation I got an infected lip so I had to be on strong painkillers and antibiotics. I was really scared the first time I had a general anaesthetic in case I didn't wake up again, but I am OK with them now. Since then I have had a few general anaesthetics with no problems.

Ever since being at secondary school I started having problems with not being able to get to the toilet in time so I had to start wearing pads which had to gradually get thicker. Through the years Alex and I have seen quite a lot of incontinence advisers at our local Ilkeston hospital who have given us alarms or specially absorbent pants which haven't always been absorbent enough.

In June 2014 I decided to try Botox on my bladder to stop it from spasming so much. I had Botox on my bladder on a Wednesday but by the Friday I started with an acute urine infection in the afternoon where I was in agony as it hurt to sit down. I tried taking painkillers with no success and all I wanted to do by teatime was go to hospital so I had to use the 111 service. They eventually got me an appointment at Ilkeston hospital at 9.00 at night. The doctor I saw gave me Amoxicillin antibiotics which Mum thought (hoped) would make me a lot better by the Sunday but this wasn't to be. On Monday I went back to the doctors and they gave me a course of Augmentin antibiotics which I have previously had but they didn't work either. By this point I was sleeping a lot, about 20 hours a day, on a lot of painkillers and drinking like a fish. When I went to my check up at the hospital where I had the Botox they found I had gone into Urine Retention so they catheterised me and said I should be much better now—I wish. I started on a new lot of antibiotics which upset my stomach a lot. By this time I had had enough and Mum didn't know what else to do for me. Luckily the following week (week 3) I had a Diabetic clinic appointment to see the consultant who, at Mum's request, admitted me there and then. I was then in hospital on a drip and a catheter for 11 days where Mum stopped with me the whole time. Whilst in hospital they gave me IV antibiotics and painkillers. We found out when I was discharged that I had Ecoli Sepsis which was why I was so poorly.

When I went back home I was better than I had been but still very weak and had the catheter in until the start of December. Mum then had to catheterise me every 4 hours as I couldn't do this myself. At the end of December I started having to go to the toilet a lot at night—up to 5 times an hour. By the 7th January 2015 I was gaunt as I had hardly slept for the last fortnight. When I saw the Urologist he put a catheter in for me for long term use. Despite having the catheter in I was still bypassing and I got one infection a month where I had to have antibiotics. In July I had an operation to have a Supra Pubic Catheter put in and some more Botox as this would decrease the number of infections and stop me from bypassing until the Botox wore off again.

Other Didmoad problems

When I was about 17 years old I started having problems with my sodium level being low so I had to restrict my fluid intake and my desmopressin tablets (DDAVP) which was really hard as I was thirsty all the time. My Diabetes consultant at the time suggested that I try only taking 1 desmopressin a day at weekends so I could take more during the week. One day I tried cutting down to 2 tablets but I couldn't cope as I was too thirsty and going to the toilet a lot. I also tried taking sodium tablets but the problem with these was that they made me thirstier so this wasn't a good idea either. Since then I have had to have my sodium level checked every time I go to the Diabetic clinic (every 4 months) and in between if I think it needs checking because I am either too thirsty or think it might be low. Now I have to have a drink at set times and only have a small cup (150 ml) so that I can keep track of how much I am drinking.

In the past I have tried taking tablets to help with my irritable bladder but they had the side effect of causing a dry mouth. When I am really thirsty I try sucking ice cubes which Mum keeps in the freezer all year round just in case. As a consequence of not being able to drink much, (1200 ml a day) I have problems with emptying my bowel very well or suffering from a split anus. To try and counteract this problem I have had a laxative which worked for a while but then they changed the recipe and this made me thirsty and was too much for my bowel. I now cope as best as I can with these combined problems.

These aren't the only problems though! Since 2014 when I had Ecoli Sepsis I have not been able to walk as far as I did before, because of my deteriorating energy levels and balance so I have to take a wheelchair with me when we go out for a walk so I can sit a bit and walk a bit. Now I am severely deaf in my left ear and profoundly deaf in my right ear so without my hearing aids in I can hardly hear a thing. The only good side of being deaf is that noises at night, like rain and bangs outside, like fireworks, don't wake me up. The hearing aids I wear are the strongest on the market and there isn't much scope for turning them up but they say my hearing is too good for a cochlea implant... grrr! Now I am totally blind and when I take my hearing aids out I can't hear a thing. When Mum washes my hair for me she will communicate with me by using the deaf blind manual where you sign on the other person's hand. I suffer from getting eczema on my scalp and down my ear canal which I use cream for. Having eczema down my ear canal when I wear my hearing aids all the time makes my ears very itchy so I get a lot of ear infections. To try and counteract this problem I have my ears cleaned out every 6 weeks or so at our local hospital. When I have my ears cleaned out I am surprised they can't see light coming through the other side! When I get ear infections or sore ears I have to leave one or both of my hearing aids out making it difficult to hear!

I can't go out on my own because of my poor balance and even inside the house where I know where everything is I still sometimes fall over because of my poor balance, so I have two Zimmer frames around to help me if I fall. I suffer a little from Startle Myoclonus where my arm sometimes jerks for which I take Epilim.

I suffer with Gastric Reflux for which I take Esomeprazol and take Gaviscon after every meal. In the evenings when Dad gives me the Gaviscon, he will say, "Open the garage door," when he wants me to open my mouth, which always makes me smile. When Mum wants me to open my mouth so she can give me the Gaviscon, she will say, "Open sesame," or "Ready," and Dad will say, "They aren't the words!"

For the headaches and other pains I suffer with a lot I take Gabapentin which help to take the pain away. With all the tablets I have to take I am surprised I don't rattle!

As a result of the Chronic Fatigue I sleep for about 12 hours most nights and have a 2 hour sleep in the day just to keep me going otherwise I can't keep doing what I want to.

With coping with all of this I don't have enough time to work when I am not too tired. To keep me busy I go to my friend Shirley's house once a week where I either do Braille with her or we cook together, go to my school teacher's house to make cards or cook and go to the gym near me. On Fridays I mainly walk round Tesco's with Mum doing the shopping where I remember what Mum needs to buy like a walking - talking - notepad. I am also very good at working out dates like when we go to hospital appointments so I am also Mum's walking - talking - calendar. Another of my uses is being Mum's address book as I have a very good memory for postcodes and telephone numbers.

Chapter 15

Alex

I have tried really hard throughout my book to keep what I write about me, even though Alex and I have been so close right from being little, so it has been really hard work! But now I will tell you a bit more about Alex.

At secondary school Alex always got on well with the teachers, having a good joke with them even to the point of being cheeky. When Alex first got to school he always used to go for a walk before school started and meet up with the teachers before they started work. Once, when he walked up the drive that runs between the two blocks at school he met up with Mr Hezelgrave and he asked Mr Hezelgrave, "How is the old banger?" meaning their car, which was very old and Mr Hezelgrave said, "Oh Mrs Hezelgrave is fine thanks."

Mrs Hezelgrave also worked at the school. One morning, Alex met up with Mrs Hezelgrave and she told Alex that Mr Hezelgrave had tried giving her a fright to get rid of the hiccups, but nothing had worked, so Alex asked, "Have you tried looking in the mirror?" and Mrs Hezelgrave hit him and said, "Yes, I have looked in the mirror at my beautiful face" and Alex said, "Yes, whatever," and she hit him again. She then said to Alex, "I'm not supposed to hit students," and Alex said, "Oh don't worry about it. I am used to it."

Once when the visually impairment base was really short staffed Alex helped out. Mrs Hezelgrave walked in and asked Alex if she could have so many copies of a worksheet doing using the photo copier, expecting Alex to do it, but Alex said, "Sure, the photo copier is over there Miss!" In other words, do it yourself. When Mrs Hezelgrave told another member of staff about this, she did admit that Alex was busy but she didn't expect Alex to just come out and say it!

At junior school there was a Support Assistant called Mrs Simpson who used to really wind Alex up. When Alex left junior school he thought, "Oh good, no more Mrs Simpson" but when he started at secondary school, who should go down to fetch him from his taxi, but Mrs Simpson and he thought, "Oh here we go again!" Once in a lesson, Mrs Simpson forgot to take something, so Alex went back to the visually impairment base to get it. On the way out of the room Mrs Simpson shouted, "Can't be perfect all the time Alex," and Alex replied, "Some of the time would be a start Miss!"

Once in biology Mrs Simpson supported Alex and when they were talking about something with the rest of the group Alex made a cheeky comment to Mrs Simpson and his biology teacher said, "Did you hear that Mrs Simpson," and she said, "Yes I did, comments off Alex like that just go in one ear and out the other," and she nudged Alex and said, "And why is that?" and Alex replied, "Because there is nothing in the middle to stop it," and she said, "I knew he was going to say that!"

Alex was once a little late for a French lesson, so when he entered the classroom his teacher asked him, "Ca va?" and Alex replied, "Non. Je suis knackered," and Mrs Bitten his teacher replied, "Don't you mean "Je suis fatigue"" through laughing, and Alex replied, "Non. Je suis knackered," making everybody laugh. Throughout his life Alex was always like that: his humour was second to none!

Up until about 5 years ago Alex was happy living at home with us and just having time to himself when we went on holiday, but about 5 years ago he started thinking about moving out. The first few properties that Alex was shown were all bungalows which Alex really objected to! We also heard from social services who had been there when Alex was shown the property that they weren't big enough for what Alex would need. At the time Alex also had worries about whether he could afford to live on his own, with care, so he went off the idea for a while.

In 2014 Alex again decided to put his name down on a housing list without Mum or I knowing about it. The first thing we knew was when the social worker rang and asked if Alex still wanted to live independently as there was a new-build house available, so Mum had to ring and ask Alex as he was out. Not long after Alex had confirmed he wanted to live independently, Mum and Alex got to go and have a look at the new-build house and it was great. In early September Alex went to sign the contract for the house and started moving all his stuff in. It was good that Alex had time before he actually moved in so he could get all the appliances and furniture ordered and delivered. The only trouble with him signing the contract so early was that he had to pay rent even before he could move in. He had to wait for all the care to be funded and arranged before he could move in and this wasn't until December! Since Alex needed 24/7 care he would need a carer during the day and a nurse at night. Alex had been used to having different carers each day when he was at home but unfortunately social services would only fund a live-in carer. The Health Service would only fund specially trained carers instead of nurses. Whilst Alex was still at home Mediline (the caring agency he used), sent the carers that were to be with Alex at night when he moved in, to our house to receive training from the nurses we had. Since Alex was receiving specially trained carers instead of nurses the Health Service would only fund me to have a nurse once a week and specially trained carers the rest of the time.

Once Alex did move out he enjoyed the independence it gave him, but it was a rocky road as he had to get used to having a carer as a live-in and they had to get used to looking after Alex. The Care Agency couldn't always meet Alex's needs and sometimes the carers they sent weren't trained up enough. On some occasions the carers had heavy accents and Alex couldn't understand them because of his deafness, but the agency had nobody else that they could send.

In September Mum, Dad and I went on holiday down to Devon for two weeks which we really enjoyed. Whilst we were on holiday Mum kept in touch with Alex, phoning him in the morning and at night. Mum noticed when she spoke to Alex that he was starting with a bad cough and she said to him that he sounded like he was starting with a chest infection and he needed to get an appointment at the doctors, but Alex said he was all right it was just catarrh. When we got back from the holiday (on Alex's birthday) he came to see us and he seemed OK. On the Sunday we took him out for his birthday to his favourite restaurant called The Newdigate. Alex came to see us on Monday after the craft session he went to, as normal. On the Tuesday he came to see us to have a cup of tea and take a tablet. He had just been to the doctors because he had a pain in his side and the doctor gave him Tramadol painkillers thinking he might have pulled a muscle when he fell the week before and he had an appointment the next day. Unknown to us the doctor had diagnosed him with mild tachycardia and a suspected windpipe infection and he wanted to admit Alex to hospital there and then but Alex refused.

The following morning Mum rang to speak to Alex at 9.30 but Alex was still in bed as he had had a bad night. Alex's carer went to wake him up at 10 o'clock but he was unresponsive, so she did CPR for 20 minutes whilst she waited for the ambulance to get there. The carer rang Mum as soon as the ambulance came so she could come straight away. When Mum arrived the ambulance crew were using the defibrillator to try and start Alex's heart and they were trying to find a vein to give him some adrenalin. There were 4 ambulance crew working on him, one on each hand and foot, but at 11 o'clock he was pronounced dead. The ambulance crew thought he had died of a heart attack but the post mortem showed it was due to double pneumonia.

I had been out that morning but I went as soon as I could but when I got there (about 11.15) he was dead so I went and gave him a kiss and felt his face whilst I cried. Dad got there not long after me and then we had to wait for the undertakers to come and collect his body. I then began the hard work of letting everybody know about Alex's passing. There were gasps of shock and disbelief from everybody as nothing had warned us. We had the funeral about 3 weeks later. He had a good send off as there were lots of people there. We have buried some of his ashes and I will have some of my ashes going in with him when I go. Alex and I have both got a shortened life expectancy, so I never thought we would live over 40, but I never thought it would be so soon!

Alex has left a big hole in our hearts and lives that we don't know how to fill. Mum goes to visit where Alex's ashes are nearly every day and takes him some flowers. There isn't a day that goes by when we don't think of him but especially at weekends when we used to go out together and on Wednesdays when he used to come for dinner. Alex died on the 7th of the month which was a Wednesday so we don't like Wednesdays or the

7th of the month! Mum found Mother's Day really hard and she didn't want to celebrate her birthday without Alex! I try and keep myself busy so I don't have too long to think about it, but the pain of losing Alex is still there and walks with me every day. They say that losing somebody gets easier with time; I don't think that is necessarily true. I just think you learn to live with the changes. Writing about what happened brings it all back to me, not that I forget about it, but it just brought it all back to the front!

Chapter 16

Favourite Subjects

You will probably think from reading my book so far, that Maths is my favourite subject, but you are wrong! My favourite subject is food. When I was little Alex and I used to share a sausage roll as Alex would only eat the meat and I ate all the pastry! When I was little shops used to sell Penguin bars in a pack where there was a red, yellow, blue and green that all tasted the same but I had it in my head that I didn't like the green ones. I also had it in my head that I didn't like the crumbs of Weetabix though that was what Weetabix were made up of! I used to like savoury rice but I didn't like the peas or peppers in it, so I got Mum to pick them out for me. Kids!

Now I love my food despite having to be careful of how much sugar I have because of the diabetes. My motto has always been 'eat first and ask questions later!' Once when I went out for a meal with my Aunty Marian and Uncle Geoff, the meal I ordered came and there was a lot of food, so they thought that half of it would be theirs but I kept ploughing through it. When I had finished eating, my Uncle Geoff said to me, "It must cost a fortune to feed you!" When I got home and told Dad he said he was right, it does cost a fortune to feed you! I love trying different types of food whether I am in or out but I have to be careful not to eat anything too spicy or salty, like Chinese as it makes me too thirsty.

Another of my favourite subjects is puzzles and word games. I love playing scrabble either just for fun or competitively which I can do because I have a Braille scrabble board and tiles. Mum and I do crosswords by Mum reading the clue out to me, telling me how many letters it is and what letters are in it. I also do the code words where Mum will tell me what the string of numbers are and if there is a letter in the word and I will get Mum to count certain numbers and fill in the letter for me. I like to do crosswords when I go to the hospital for appointments (of which I have quite a few) to pass the time. When I was still in the Paediatrics Diabetic clinic I used to enjoy playing the water games where you had things floating around in the water that you had to get in a certain place by pressing a button. Mum, Dad and I all play cards whilst on holiday using my Braille and print cards.

I have just bought myself a Braillenote on which I use to read books, write my book and other documents and there are games on here. There is internet explorer, email, calendar, address book, scientific calculator and file manager on it that I know how to use too.

I often think back to things that weren't there when I was little and it makes me feel really old, at least 40! I remember roads that were built after I was born that I know of, the first time 24 hour telly came on, before I had a video collection and other things. I especially feel old when I think of all I have been through during my life and all that I have done so far.

Life has presented me with a lot of challenges but I still keep plodding on. My favourite sayings are:
I am caught between the devil and the deep blue sea;
Stuck between a rock and a hard place; and
The only way is up.
Which all amounts to the same thing. Carry on as best as you can!

Yes, I have a short life expectancy, but nobody knows what is round the corner do they? So, que sera, sera - whatever will be, will be!

The end.